# Reading
# Instruction for
# the Adult Illiterate

# Reading
# Instruction for

---

# the Adult Illiterate

*Edward V. Jones*

American Library Association

*Chicago 1981*

**pp. 45, 45–46**
Extracts from "Counseling the Disadvantaged Boy," by Jesse E. Gordon, in Amos and Grambs, *Counseling the Disadvantaged Youth,* © 1968. Reprinted by permission of Prentice-Hall, Inc., Englewood Cliffs, New Jersey.

**pp.58–59**
Extract from *Comprehension and Learning: A Conceptual Framework for Teachers* by Frank Smith. Copyright © 1975 by Holt, Rinehart and Winston. Reprinted by permission of Holt, Rinehart and Winston.

**p. 61**
Extract from "A Psycholinguistic View of the Fluent Reading Process," by Charles Cooper and Anthony Petrosky, *Journal of Reading* (Dec. 1976). Reprinted by permission of the authors and the International Reading Association.

**p. 62**
List of "nonwords" adapted from "Familiarity of Letter Sequences and Tachistoscopic Identification," by G. A. Miller, J. S. Brunner and L. Postman, *Journal of General Psychology* 50: 129–30 (1954). Used by permission.

**pp. 110, 111–12**
Extracts from *Classroom Reading Instruction: Alternative Approaches* by Cunningham, Arthur and Cunningham (Lexington, Mass.: D. C. Heath and Co., 1977).

**pp. 112–13**
Extract from George D. and Evelyn B. Spache, *Reading in the Elementary School*, fourth edition. Copyright © 1977 by Allyn and Bacon, Inc., Boston. Reprinted with permission.

**p. 115**
Extract from *Teaching Reading Vocabulary*, by Dale D. Johnson and P. David Pearson. Copyright © 1978 by Holt, Rinehart and Winston. Reprinted by permission of Holt, Rinehart and Winston.

**pp. 125–26**
Extract from "Initiating Sustained Silent Reading," by Robert A. McCracken, *Journal of Reading* (May 1971). Reprinted by permission of Robert A. McCracken and the International Reading Association.

**p. 158**
Extract from *I Never Told Anybody: Teaching People in a Nursing Home to Write Poetry*, by Kenneth Koch. Copyright © 1977 by Alfred A. Knopf; a Vintage book published by Random House.

### Library of Congress Cataloging in Publication Data

Jones, Edward V.
   Reading instruction for the adult illiterate.

   Bibliography: p.
   Includes index.
    1.   Reading (Adult education)    2.   Illiteracy.
I.   Title.
LC5225.R4J66      428.4′2      80-23063
ISBN 0-8389-0317-7

# Contents

2168644

# Tables

# Figures

# Acknowledgments

Many people have contributed to the development of READING INSTRUCTION FOR THE ADULT ILLITERATE. Two of them, Elizabeth Bolton and Jeanne Ford, shared substantially in the preparation of the manuscript, and their ideas and suggestions are reflected in its final form. Elizabeth Bolton is the coauthor of chapter 2, the longest chapter in the book, and served as a valuable consultant throughout this project. Jeanne Ford is primarily responsible for the organization of chapter 6. As a graduate student and a fellow teacher in remedial reading classes for illiterate university employees, she also had an important influence on the overall content of the manuscript in its early stages.

All of the volunteer teachers who participated in our reading program for undereducated university employees are part of this book. In a very real sense, the plural *we*, which is employed in all uses of the first person on these pages, is a statement of fact. In addition to Jeanne Ford, our dedicated staff included Jim Henderson, Betty Louhoff, Carol Magnone, and a number of other persons who assisted for short periods. All of us owe a considerable debt of gratitude to our students, who, while they worked to better themselves, added meaning and direction to the lives of their teachers.

Another individual whose work is clearly reflected here is Carol Cooper. Her thorough and patient editing, indexing, and thoughtful criticism have made a substantial contribution to the final book.

Appreciation is also due Herbert Bloom, Senior Editor, Publishing Services of the American Library Association, and Helen Cline, Managing Editor. Without their continued guidance and encouragement, this book might never have evolved.

The author is indebted to the Adult Education Service, Department of

Education, Commonwealth of Virginia, which provided funding for his employment during 1978–1979. Some of the research undertaken in conjunction with a state-supported adult education project is reported in the first two chapters of this book.

# Introduction

READING INSTRUCTION FOR THE ADULT ILLITERATE has two distinct areas of focus: a description of adult illiterates as a segment of the population and an integrated instructional program designed to help them learn to read. For several reasons, this book is appropriate for anyone who is interested in adult remedial reading. First, a general scarcity of literature exists in the areas of adult illiteracy and the teaching of functional illiterates. Furthermore, the strategies presented in this book are based upon what is known about adult illiterates as learners and upon a consistent research-supported view of the learning-to-read process. They are not simply a smorgasbord of unrelated techniques for teaching isolated reading skills. Finally, and most importantly, these strategies *work* — and they can be easily understood by any teacher of adults, including those without prior knowledge and training in the area of reading instruction.

With respect to the adult illiterate, we offer more than a statistical tabulation. We have tried to provide some insights into the learning assets and handicaps of the undereducated adult and the conditions that he* faces in and out of the classroom in trying to learn to read. In this attempt we make no pretense of a complete psychological or sociological profile. Neither do we offer a history of illiteracy or of literacy training. Our intent is simply to highlight for the teacher (or prospective teacher) of adult illiterates some motivational and environmental factors which may particularly affect the classroom performance of adult remedial readers or, at the very least,

*Throughout this book the masculine personal pronouns have been used. They should be understood, however, to refer to members of both sexes.

some areas where the backgrounds, experiences, and expectations of teachers and learners are apt to differ.

With respect to instructional strategies, we contend that a language-based curriculum, especially for beginning adult readers, offers the best prospect for learning success. Furthermore, the language-based strategies which we describe best protect the student against the possibility of failure in the early stages of instruction. For the most part, these strategies are not unique to our program, though we have modified some methods designed for children in order to make them more suitable for adults. The fact that many of the strategies we discuss have been generally described in the literature addressed to those who teach children and employed successfully in many programs, with both children and adults, is added evidence — beyond our own experience — that they work and that they can be easily understood.

We have borrowed purposefully and selectively from other authors and synthesized from the reading and adult education literature, as well as from our own work with adult illiterates. The organization of strategies which we describe evolves from our best insight into the nature of the adult functional illiterate and from a consistent and unified view of the learning-to-read process. Our approach differs from that of the majority of reading texts, especially those for adults, which simply overview and describe a variety of teaching methods. Often these methods fail to relate to any consistent or unifying view of what learning to read entails, and they may be based upon conflicting underlying assumptions.

The task of teaching adult illiterates to read is often far more complicated than teaching children. The majority of any typical group of elementary children eventually learns — whatever the particular methods used to instruct them. This success is due in many cases not to the choice of methods but to the diligence of the teacher, the motivation of the students, and the fact that a considerable amount of time is available. For adult illiterates, a different situation exists. Since these persons have not learned to read, they are not typical learners. They have demonstrated that they do not learn easily, at least in their efforts to abstract meaning from printed symbols. Since they need to learn to read in order to pursue specific life goals, time is at a premium. They may also be hampered by insecurities and negative self-concepts with respect to their ability to learn. It thus becomes especially crucial in the case of the adult illiterate that instruction be organized in the simplest and most logical manner. The learner must be able to relate the unfamiliar to the familiar and to process information in the most natural and least threatening way.

Consistent with the preceding rationale, our program of language-based instructional strategies reflects a holistic orientation to print. Especially for beginning readers, we emphasize a full context of printed language, focusing upon content and syntax which are familiar to the learner. We do not focus upon isolated sound-symbol correspondences and other subskills until the student has experienced substantial success through language experience and assisted reading. Even at this point, our reinforcement exercises relate directly to contextual material to which the student has already been exposed.

Fortunately, our emphasis upon reducing complexity and abstraction for the adult illiterate simplifies the teacher's task as well. Since the instructional program which we describe does not emphasize explicit teaching of subskills, the teacher does not need extensive training in decoding or structural analysis. In our work with functionally illiterate university employees, in fact, some of our most successful instructors had no formal training in reading at all. They were simply "experienced readers" themselves, who were motivated to help adult illiterates.

READING INSTRUCTION FOR THE ADULT ILLITERATE offers a framework for language-based reading instruction which affords the opportunity for the teacher's continued exploration and experimentation. This foundation has provided the basis for our successful work with adult illiterates. We are confident that it will do the same for our readers.

For the most part, references in this book are cited according to the format prescribed in the *Publication Manual of the American Psychological Association*. This format avoids the use of footnotes. Authors, dates of publication, and page numbers of direct quotations are cited in context. Complete references can be located in the bibliography.

# Part 1

# A Profile of
# the Adult Illiterate

# Chapter 1

# The Scope of Illiteracy

Before we discuss instructional programs for adult remedial readers, it is necessary to put the adult illiteracy problem in perspective. This first chapter thus addresses several general but important questions. Who is the adult illiterate? How can this term be defined? How many adult illiterates are there? What is the cost of illiteracy, both to the individual adult illiterate and to society? What sorts of programs exist for adult remedial readers? How many persons are helped by these programs, compared to the number of persons who need this help? What is the quality of help received? These questions are of course difficult to answer in a manner which is accurately reflective of all programs and localities. We hope, however, that our discussion will provide perspective and insight into understanding functional illiteracy in the United States as a complex social problem.

The first major section of this chapter traces the recent evolution in definitions and social interpretations of the term *illiterate* and how different conceptualizations have produced varying statistical representations of the magnitude of the illiteracy problem. The emphasis here is upon the comparatively recent trend of identifying and tabulating illiterates in terms of their functional deficiencies in literacy-related areas. We focus upon several recent efforts to identify and categorize undereducated adults in this manner.

The second and third major sections focus upon the cost of illiteracy and the scope of current programs in adult remedial reading and Adult Basic Education. The cost of illiteracy is discussed in terms of both human and economic factors. The scope of programs is reviewed with respect to sponsors, enrollment levels, educational outcomes, and financial costs and rewards.

## Definitions, Interpretations, and Statistics

On the surface, the concept of illiteracy seems easy to understand. A person who is illiterate, as the term is generally defined, is a person who is unable to read and write. The key issue then becomes unable to read and write *what,* or to what extent?

### Grade-Level Standards for Functional Illiteracy

In recent years illiteracy rates in the United States have often been inferred from tabulations relating to years of formal education completed. This occurred first in the late 1940s, when it was assumed by the U.S. Bureau of the Census that virtually all illiterates would be among those persons who had completed fewer than five years of school.

Similar standards for estimating illiteracy rates have been used comparatively recently. For example, a sample survey by the U.S. Bureau of the Census in 1969 found that 1.4 million persons, fourteen years of age or older (or 1 percent of persons in this age range), were illiterate. Stauffer (1973) comments as follows on how illiterates were tabulated in this survey.

> To be counted as an illiterate in this survey, the respondent must first have declared himself to have completed less than the sixth grade in school, and then stated that he cannot read or write a simple message in any language. Therefore, not counted were all persons who were literate in a foreign language, but knew little or no English, and all those that completed six or more years of school but who still could not read or write. [p. 253]

Not only is grade level in general an undependable indicator of reading ability, but also the literacy skills required to function in the 1980s have far surpassed those which parallel a grade school education. Such everyday reading demands as applications of various types, bank and medical forms, contracts, and income tax and insurance forms reflect readability levels ranging from tenth grade up. While a fifth or sixth grade standard for literacy may have been reasonably accurate at one time, this is no longer the case. The literacy requirements of modern living have increased as society has grown more complex.

If, as seems reasonably the case, high school grade levels provide a more accurate index of functional literacy, the 1.4 million figure rises substantially. According to the 1970 Census, there were at that time 54.3 million adults who had not gone beyond the eleventh grade (Jhin, 1977). Cook

(1977) states that there are approximately 31 million U.S. citizens twenty-five years of age or older who do not have a ninth grade education.

## Specific Problems with Grade-Level and Self-Report Standards

Although persons in the United States who have had limited years of schooling are to some extent the same persons who might be classified as functionally illiterate, the tabulations of these two groups are only rough approximations of each other. For a variety of reasons, "grade in school completed" is not an adequate indicator of functional literacy level. Neither (always) are the individual's self-reports about whether he can read or not.

In most instances a grade-level cutoff provides an underestimate of persons who cannot read and write well enough to meet the literacy demands of modern living. The author has taught twelfth grade remedial English "students" (subsequently high school graduates) who virtually could not read and write and a substantial number of others who were scarcely "independent" in terms of functional literacy skills. They could not read aloud even very basic materials, or comprehend them from print.

A further difficulty with the "grade completed" standard for adult literacy is the effect of disuse. If, for example, an adult could read at sixth grade level when he was in school (whatever this standard is taken to mean), there is little likelihood that he can still do so unless he has continued to read at a level that challenges him. Ironically, it is most often persons with borderline literacy skills who are apt to let these skills diminish. This is not surprising, perhaps, when one considers that persons with the fewest years of formal schooling are most apt to be the products of social environments where school and school subjects are least emphasized. These persons are also most apt to be employed in situations where reading needs are minimized. In any case, literacy skills are apt to diminish as time passes after an individual's school attendance. It is possible, of course, that the reverse may occur: one may improve his literacy skills after leaving school. For this to happen, however, the individual must have exceptional self-discipline and opportunities of a type not usually present in the environments of the disadvantaged.

Another problem with the grade-equivalent standard for measuring literacy stems from the difficulties inherent in the process of gathering accurate information from individuals through surveys and Census reports. In general, people tend not to report accurately information they believe that investigators may perceive as reflecting negatively on them. On the other hand, some persons may try to attract sympathy to their plight, or may genuinely underestimate their abilities, reporting that they cannot read at all, when in fact they have nominal literacy skills. Thus there is often reason to question the reliability of interviewees' direct statements as to their grade levels and reading competencies.

Even when grade levels are accurately reported (as already observed), they may provide little insight into what individuals can accomplish in terms of functional literacy *applications*. With the growing complexities of modern society, it has become apparent that literacy should be defined and illiteracy rates tabulated in terms of persons' abilities to meet real-life reading and writing demands.

## Illiteracy as Functional Deficiency

Several research projects have been undertaken during the last decade to explore the functional reading competencies of adults in the United States. Noteworthy among these are two studies by Louis Harris and Associates, Inc., in 1970 and 1971, and the four-year Adult Performance Level Project, conducted at the University of Texas 1971–75.

Louis Harris and Associates were commissioned by the National Reading Council in 1970 and by the National Reading Center in 1971 to assess the functional reading abilities of adults in the United States. For this purpose, Harris employed instrumentation based upon a variety of practical "survival" materials, such as applications of various types, income tax forms, telephone dialing instructions for long-distance calls, etc. The findings of both Harris studies suggest that at the beginning of the 1970s there were between 15 million and 20 million adults — persons 16 years of age and older — who were seriously impaired in their ability to respond to print in real-life situations. The statement of purpose for the 1970 study includes the following pronouncement, which helps to distinguish both Harris studies from previous efforts to measure literacy rates.

> From its inception the study was planned to measure the "survival" literacy rate in the United States. It would determine the percentage of Americans lacking the functional or practical reading skills necessary to "survive" in this country. How many Americans were prevented by reading deficiencies, we asked ourselves, from filling out application forms for such common needs as a social security number, a personal bank loan, Public Assistance, Medicaid, a driver's license? Fundamentally this is a study of functional rather than by-rote literacy. [p. 1]

Subjects in Harris's 1970 study were instructed to read and fill out five application forms pertaining to the above areas. Persons who were unable to respond meaningfully to 90 percent (10 percent incorrect answers) of the items on these forms (combined) were judged to have a literacy level described as "marginal survival threshold." On the basis of their sampling technique, involving a dozen interviews each in more than 100 locations throughout the country, Harris and Associates assigned this rating to 18.5 million adults in the United States. Lower ratings — questionable survival threshold (20 percent or more incorrect answers) and low survival threshold (30 percent or more incorrect answers) — were assigned to 7.1 million and 4.3 million of the same adults. Therefore, depending upon the level of survival employed, the range of illiteracy was judged to be from 3 percent (the percentage of subjects who averaged more than 30 percent incorrect) to 13 percent (the percentage who averaged more than 10 percent incorrect) of the U.S. adult population.

Further analysis of the Harris and Associates 1970 data suggests a number of additional generalizations that characterize the functionally illiterate segment of the population. A slightly higher proportion of illiterates, according to this study, are rural dwellers than are city dwellers. Small cities and towns have an even better literacy record, while suburban residents are the least likely to be illiterate. The South has the highest rate of illiteracy and the West has the lowest. Illiteracy is universally associated with low income levels. Women are less likely to be illiterate than men, and the 16–24 age group has the lowest rate of illiteracy, while persons over 50 have the highest.

The 1971 study by Harris and Associates continued the emphasis on measuring functional reading ability begun in the 1970 study. The following excerpt from the statement of purpose of the latter study reflects an expansion of the format employed in 1970, based upon the same rationale.

> The study measured the ability of Americans to respond to practical, real-life situations by asking them to read and respond to the following printed material relevant to the lives of many Americans:
> — Direct-dialing instructions of a telephone directory that instructs people on placing long-distance phone calls without the assistance of an operator.
> — Classified employment and housing advertisements taken from newspapers across the nation that alert people to job and housing opportunities.
> — An application form designed from a variety of application forms common to the lives of many Americans that are required to qualify for a wide range of social benefits and opportunities (Social Security, public assistance, Medicare, Unemployment Benefits, credit, etc.). [p. 1]

The printed matter pertaining to direct-dialing instructions presented to subjects in the Harris firm's survey is included in figure 1. As with other material to which they were exposed, subjects were told that the clarity of the printed matter, rather than their own reading abilities, was being tested.

In addition to "measuring and analyzing" the ability of Americans to read material related to each of these functional areas, Harris and Associates' 1971 undertaking was important in another key respect. The Harris

Area Codes for Some Cities

| Place | Area Code |
|---|---|
| Evansville, Indiana | 812 |
| Oakland, California | 415 |
| Harrison, New York | 914 |
| Williamsport, Pennsylvania | 717 |
| Austin, Texas | 512 |

How to Dial

Listen to dial tone, then dial as follows:

Station-to-Station Calls
Local call . . . . . . . . . .dial local number
Long distance call . . . . dial "1" + area code + local number

Person-to-Person Calls
Dial "0" [OPERATOR], then continue to dial the number as above. [An Operator will answer to help complete your call.]

Charges for Calls (Initial 3 minutes)
Station-to-Station

|  | Day | Night | Weekend | All Days, All Hours |
|---|---|---|---|---|
| Boston, Mass. | .70 | .55 | .40 | 1.10 |
| Minneapolis, Minn. | .55 | .40 | .35 | .85 |
| Seattle, Wash. | .80 | .65 | .55 | 1.25 |

Four questions (1c, 1d, 1e and 1f) related to the information contained on the show card (above):

1c.    "Please look at this card and see if you can tell me the area code for Williamsport, Pennsylvania."

1d.    "Please look at the card again and tell me which city you could reach by dialing area code 812."

1e.    "If you wanted to place a long distance, *station-to-station* call to a friend in Austin, Texas, without the help of an operator, what would you dial? You will find the instructions on how to dial on the card."

1f.    "Please look at the card one last time and tell me the charges for a three-minute station-to-station call to Seattle, Washington, at night."

*Source:* Louis Harris and Associates, Inc. *Survival Literary Study* (1970). ERIC Document No. ED 068 813.

Figure 1. Direct-Dialing Instructions

firm compiled all the items on the study questionnaire into an index "to be used on a regular basis as a measure of functional reading problems in the United States." Although we are not aware that this index has been or will be used on a regular basis, it provides the potential for analysis of literacy trends in a manner not attempted before 1970. The fact that the Harris index has not been employed more extensively is perhaps due in part to the Adult Performance Level Project, which began the same year as the 1971 study. The original APL Project and the various smaller-scale undertakings it has inspired have provided materials and increased interest in measuring literacy in functional contexts.

## Adult Performance Level Project

The original Adult Performance Level (APL) Project was a comprehensive four-year undertaking, conducted at the University of Texas and funded by the U.S. Office of Education in the early 1970s. The project initially involved a national survey on functional level competency in reading (as well as other areas) and, subsequently, development of a curriculum to meet the needs identified in this survey. A number of states have now adopted the APL framework and modified it to meet their own objectives.

Although the implications which can be derived from the original APL Project are similar to (though more pessimistic than) those drawn from the Harris studies, the APL effort is broader in scope, including, but not restricted to, literacy issues in the purest sense. The following discussion will thus be concerned with a wider spectrum, termed "functional competence." The emphasis is upon how the APL designers developed and measured this construct, as well as what they determined about the functional abilities of the U.S. adult population.

We begin our discussion by focusing upon the Adult Performance Level Project's introductory statement from its 1975 publication, *Adult Functional Competency: A Summary.*

> The ability to use skills and knowledge with the functional competence needed for meeting the requirements of adult living is often called "functional literacy," "survival literacy," or, occasionally, "coping skills." The central objectives of the Adult Performance Level (APL) project are to specify the competencies which are functional to economic and educational success in today's society and to develop devices for assessing those competencies of the adult population of the United States.
>
> Although millions, perhaps billions, of dollars have been spent on educational research, practically all of that money has been in support of studies designed to either develop educational programs or products or to compare the effectiveness or efficiency of competing programs and products. Unfortunately, questions of effectiveness and efficiency are irrelevant if the objectives on which the programs are based are not appropriate.

Attempts to use the tools of behavioral and operations research to specify the transcendent objectives of educational systems have been practically nonexistent. Researchers are much more adept at answering the question, "Which reading program is most effective?" than the more fundamental question, "Why is reading important?" The Adult Performance Level project activities occur in the latter arena.   [p. 1]

Several aspects of this statement deserve comment. Of particular significance is the assertion that "questions of effectiveness and efficiency are irrelevant if the objectives on which programs are based are not appropriate." This statement takes on added importance in light of the information that the Adult Performance Level Project is more concerned with "why reading is important" than "which reading program is most effective." The combined implication of these statements seems to be that many programs both teach reading and measure reading success by inappropriate or meaningless standards. In short, reading ability can only be evaluated in terms of the extent to which the individual is able to contend successfully with his living requirements.

Although the rationale described above does not differ appreciably from that underlying the reading competence concept of Harris and Associates, the APL designers went to greater lengths to establish what real-life reading demands (and other types of real-life demands) actually are. To accomplish this, they pursued "four simultaneous lines" of inquiry:

1. Review of related literature and research.
2. Survey of state and federal agencies and foundations.
3. Conferences on adult needs.
4. Semi-structured interviews with undereducated and unemployed persons.

As a result of these activities, a "taxonomy of adult needs" was developed "which finally came to be called general knowledge areas" (p. 2). These broad areas, considered the "content of adult literacy," were labeled (1) consumer economics, (2) occupational (or occupationally related) knowledge, (3) community resources, (4) health, and (5) government and law. In conjunction with these areas, representing the content of literacy, four sets of literacy skills were identified: (1) communication skills (reading, writing, speaking, and listening), (2) computation skills, (3) problem-solving skills, and (4) interpersonal relations skills. The interrelationship between the content areas and skills, as designed by the APL staff, is reproduced as figure 2.

The next phase of the APL Project involved "specification of competencies" and "development of performance indicators" for the designated content areas and skills. After these had been laboriously field tested and revised, the national assessment of competency was administered (with

| | Consumer Economics | Occupational Knowledge | Health | Community Resources | Government and Law |
|---|---|---|---|---|---|
| Reading | Reading a newspaper grocery ad | | | | |
| Writing | Writing a grocery list | | | | |
| Speaking, Listening, Viewing | Listening to an advertise- ment on the radio | | | | |
| Computation | Computing the unit price of a grocery item | | | | |
| Problem Solving | Determin- ing the best stores in which to shop | | | | |
| Interpersonal Relations | Interacting with sales clerk suc- cessfully | | | | |

Source: *Adult Functional Competency: A Summary* (Adult Performance Level Project, 1975).

Figure 2. APL Model of Functional Competency

the assistance of Opinion Research Contractor, Princeton, N.J., as subcontractor) to a series of representative independent samples of adults "drawn from the continental United States, excluding Alaska and Hawaii." In March 1975, the assessment had been administered to five samples, each of at least 1,500 persons, or a total of over 7,500 adults. Competency levels were then established in a manner described by the Project staff as follows:

> In essence, the nationally representative survey data are used to develop "competency profiles" which are associated with different levels of adult success as measured by income, job status, and education. Three such levels have been chosen and are called simply APL 1, APL 2, and APL 3.   [p. 4]

The three APLs were labeled "adults who function with difficulty" (APL 1), "functional adults" (APL 2), and "proficient adults" (APL 3). Adults whose mastery of competency objectives fell generally at the APL 1 level were found, on the whole, to have inadequate income (poverty level or less), inadequate education (eight or fewer years of school), and to be unemployed or have jobs of low status. The percentages of the adult population which function at all three APL levels are reported in table 1, which is reproduced from the project's summary report. Although proportions differ for different content areas and skills, it can be generally observed that approximately one-fifth of the U.S. adult population is "functioning with difficulty" in reading and writing, as well as in other areas less precisely associated with literacy. Although this 20 percent can be broken down in various ways, producing a number of demographic generalizations similar to those derived from the Harris data, the message is clear. When measured by functional standards, a large number of American adults — perhaps 23 million, according to the APL study — were judged to have severe literacy deficiencies in the mid-1970s.

TABLE 1. ADULT FUNCTIONAL COMPETENCIES

| AREAS | APL COMPETENCY LEVELS | | |
|---|---|---|---|
| | 1 | 2 | 3 |
| Occupational Knowledge | 19.1 | 31.9 | 49.0 |
| Consumer Economics | 29.4 | 33.0 | 37.6 |
| Government and Law | 25.8 | 26.2 | 48.0 |
| Health | 21.3 | 30.3 | 48.3 |
| Community Resources | 22.6 | 26.0 | 51.4 |
| Reading | 21.7 | 32.2 | 46.1 |
| Problem Solving | 28.0 | 23.4 | 48.5 |
| Computation | 32.9 | 26.3 | 40.8 |
| Writing | 16.4 | 25.5 | 58.1 |
| Overall Competency Levels | 19.7 | 33.9 | 46.3 |

Source: *Adult Functional Competency: A Summary* (Adult Performance Level Project, 1975), p. 6.

## The Growth of Functional Illiteracy

The concept of functional illiteracy, as measured by Harris and Associates and Adult Performance Level Studies, is extremely important. While statistics indicate that the number of complete illiterates has dropped considerably (and consistently) since 1900, the extent of functional illiteracy is growing. Although a variety of explanations have been offered for this fact, the essence of the problem is stated by Lauren Resnick, a University of Pittsburgh psychologist, as quoted in *Newsweek*: "This is really a crisis of rising standards. . . . We're working on the problem of how to make people learn to live with print" (1978). As people have grown in their abilities to cope with rudimentary reading tasks, the literacy demands of society have increased at a much greater rate, leaving many individuals worse off than before.

By whatever standard it is measured, the undereducated population spans a large cross-section of American society. According to a 1969 Census survey (which, though it underestimates the problem, allows some inferences as to its distribution), hard-core illiteracy among whites in the United States was at that time 0.7 percent, while the percentage for blacks was approximately 3.6 (Patterson, 1977). The most literacy-impoverished ethnic groups in the United States are Mexican Americans and Puerto Ricans. Of these two groups, 45 percent of the adult population, according to the 1969 survey, had less than an eighth grade education and 75 percent were not high school graduates.

Data provided by the National Advisory Council on Adult Education suggest that as recently as 1974 more than half of the adult population twenty-five years of age or older of nine states, all in the South, had less than a high school education and were not enrolled in school. At the same time, all fifty states and the District of Columbia had comparable groups of undereducated adults, comprising at least 25 percent of their total populations. Many of these persons (probably over 20 percent in the South, for example) had not completed eighth grade. The number of illiterates in the older segment of the population is disproportionately high (Hunter and Harman, 1979). A majority of adult illiterates are more than fifty-five years of age.

The individual adult illiterate is about equally likely to be white or nonwhite (Smith and Martin, 1972). A much larger portion of the nonwhite population is educationally deficient, though in the case of American blacks the median level of school years completed has increased dramatically from 5 years 8 months in 1970 to 11 years in 1975 (Hunter and Harman, 1979). Based on these figures, the difference between whites and blacks in median years of formal education completed is now negligible.

While the preceding statistics reflect varying definitions of literacy and functional competence, they also reveal the scope and diversity of functional illiteracy in the United States.

# The Cost of Illiteracy

The cost of illiteracy in the United States can be discussed conceptually in two dimensions. Illiteracy can be viewed in terms of its cost to the individual and the family of the individual who cannot read or write. It can also be considered in terms of its impact as a social problem and economic burden upon society as a whole. Although analysis of neither dimension lends itself to precise measures — either of human or financial cost — the following discussion may provide insight into the extensive consequences and implications of the illiteracy problem.

The plight of the illiterate in a nation of advanced technology is far different from that of the undereducated in developing nations. As John Stauffer (1973) observes:

> The illiterate in the United States is an anachronism. He does not fit into this time or place, for his economic functions are now minimal and being rapidly displaced by the mechanisms of an advanced technology. Because his numbers and functions are both relatively small, he is unknown to most and ignored by many. [p. 252]

While the rate of illiteracy in the United States may seem insignificant compared to that of developing nations (well over 90 percent in many instances, depending on how illiteracy is defined), the fact of illiteracy is often a much more serious problem for the individual undereducated adult in this country. As Stauffer elaborates:

> There is no mass culture of illiteracy in the United States. It is a minority problem, affecting specific people, families, and groups. And although it is not of the numerical proportion of nations like Mali, to the illiterate minority faced with the multiple intricacies of life in the United States, it can be no less significant. [p. 252]

## Cost to the Individual Illiterate

The undereducated segment of the population has been hardest hit by automation, which has eliminated many jobs formerly held by these persons. In addition to the shrinkage in the supply of available jobs for undereducated persons, they must contend with what Stauffer terms the "socioeconomic imperatives" of a culture which tends to look down upon persons who are undereducated and/or not gainfully employed, without always being appreciative of the reasons for these conditions. Disadvantaged adults, as children, were frequently "processed out" of a "traditional middle class school system, which emphasizes middle class values and verbal skills" (Ulmer, 1972, p. 35). As adults, therefore, they are apt to live in poverty, shut off from any realistic possibility of advancement.

Even for poverty, the disadvantaged and undereducated adult today pays a much greater social price than he did in previous generations.

> Whereas poverty used to be a sentimental virtue, times have changed and so have attitudes toward the poor. . . . Poverty is a stigma today, not because it is any less pitiful, but because we have invented a cure for it: education. Since a high school diploma guaranteed a person the means of earning a livelihood, many people think poverty is unnecessary. They can't understand why the poor don't get educated and go to work. What they do not realize is that the poor have tried to get an education but either failed or been rejected.   [Ulmer, p. 37]

The same theme is developed at great length by William Ryan in his aptly titled book, *Blaming the Victim* (1971). An excerpt reads:

> The prevalent belief in America is that, under normal circumstances, everyone can obtain sufficient income for the necessities of life. Those who are unable to do so are special deviant cases, persons who for one reason or another are not able to adapt themselves to the generally satisfactory income producing system. . . . All were seen, however, as personal failures.   [pp. 14–15]

It is apparent that persons who are unemployed and poor, a consequence to a large extent of their lack of education, pay a substantial price. Not only does their lack of education force them to continue to compete only for manual labor jobs, which are in shrinking supply, and often would not permit them to better themselves in the first place, but they must contend with the prejudice which other segments of society direct against them. This predicament and its accompanying damage to individual self-concepts, coupled with the diverting conditions often present in the social environments of the poor and undereducated (to be discussed in a later chapter), create a self-sustaining cycle from which it is difficult for the illiterate to escape. He is trapped by the very way of life which has caused his predicament in the first place.

In addition to the cost it exacts from the individual in terms of frustration and denial of opportunities for life fulfillment, the economic cost of educational deficiency is well documented. The *1978 CBS News Almanac* contains figures based on U.S. Bureau of Census reports relating education and income. Based upon figures stated to represent the "median income of full-time year-round workers, 25 years of age or older," the 1976 median income for males who had not completed the eighth grade was $8,647. This compares to $11,511 for males who had completed one to three years of high school and $13,542 for those who had completed high school. Corresponding figures for females in the above three categories were $5,109 (less than eighth grade), $6,355 (one to three years of high school), and $7,777 (high school graduate).

In his article "The Value of an Education," Kern Alexander (1976) puts the discrepancy even more forcefully by contrasting the monetary benefits associated with different "educational plateaus." In terms of 1972 dollars, Alexander contends that the average male with less than an eighth grade education can expect to earn $279,997 from age eighteen until death (p. 459). This figure jumps to $389,208 for persons with from one to three years' high school and to $478,873 for high school graduates. In terms of percentages, the individual with less than an eighth grade education makes only about 58 percent as much as a high school graduate.

The circumstances in which he finds himself are not lost on the functional illiterate. As Giles and Conti (1978) observe, "It is erroneous to equate illiteracy and ignorance. Disadvantaged groups are now more sophisticated than ever" (p. 62). In this age of mass media and diversified communication channels, the functional illiterate is all too aware of the disadvantages he suffers. The problem is that awareness alone is not sufficient to alleviate his difficulties.

As an individual, the adult illiterate in the United States thus faces a set of problems far different from the citizen of Mali or any other underdeveloped nation. As a member of the majority culture in an unindustrialized society, the individual Mali illiterate does not face either the competetive disadvantage or the negative attitudes that his counterpart encounters in the United States. Furthermore, he has no occasion to think of himself as a low-level member of society; he has, for the most part, the same opportunities as his peers, and he is unaware that persons in other countries are often much better off.

## Cost to Society

In addition to the consequences it exacts from large numbers of individuals and their families, illiteracy is a social problem which affects society as a whole. In this age of social welfare programs, taxpayers support those who cannot support themselves. The more persons who are functionally literate, the more who are employable. As individuals grow in their literacy skills, their employment is higher paid and more secure; they thus contribute more to the tax base. Clearly, the more persons who contribute to the tax base and the fewer who must be supported by it, the better for society as a whole and the individual taxpayer. One state which recognizes this logic is Florida, where the State Department of Education has instituted a publicity campaign based upon the theme "Illiteracy: We can't afford it." According to *Newsweek*, the ultimate annual cost of illiteracy in terms of lost tax revenues in Florida is estimated at $700 million.

In both human and economic terms, the cost of illiteracy is overwhelming. Persons whose low-level or nonexistent literacy skills prevent them from supporting themselves at better than marginal levels expand welfare roles and burden the resources of the penal system and other tax-supported institutions. This is a price society can ill afford.

# Current Efforts to Contend with Illiteracy

A number of different types of programs exist for the purpose of upgrading the literacy skills of undereducated adults. This section focuses upon the various categories of such programs and provides an overview of their supporting legislation, sponsors, and accomplishments.

## Legislation

The plight of this country's functional illiterates and other Adult Basic Education students received its first substantial legislative assistance from the Economic Opportunity Act of 1964 and the Adult Education Act of 1966. According to Edwin Smith and McKinley Martin (1972),

> Implicit in these laws is the recognition that in order to cope on a minimal level with the present and the future social and occupational conditions a person needs literacy education plus a basic core of concepts, facts, and attitudes necessary for upward mobility. This core may include orientation to the world of work, good health practices, consumer education, fundamental social science concepts, citizens rights and possibilities, and personal social development. [p. 18]

The impact of the 1966 act was substantially extended by the Adult Education Act of 1969. While the original legislation provided literacy education for persons with less than an eighth grade education, the latter act extended this opportunity to persons who had not completed the twelfth grade. This provision increased the potential number of recipients nationwide from 24 million to 69 million (Cook, 1977). The 1969 act also provided funds for programs, teacher training, and demonstration projects.

Further support for adult literacy was provided by the Education Amendments of 1974. This legislation was important because its passage accorded to reading skill what Cook (1977) terms "statutory recognition." This bill, parts of which have been administered by the Right to Read Office, is aimed at improving reading instruction for all groups of people through funding innovative reading programs and projects.

## Programs and Sponsors

In the aftermath of the Economic Opportunity Act of 1964 and the Adult Education Act of 1966, adult remedial education began to expand at an unprecedented rate. As a result of this legislation, the total enrollment in Adult Basic Education programs (primarily in public school systems) increased from 37,991 in 1965 to 377,660 in 1966 and continued to go up from that point (Coles, 1976). According to the National Advisory Council on Adult Education, in 1976 there were 3,371,265 participants in programs covered by the 1966 and 1969 acts. The term *Adult Basic Education*, as used in this book (and elsewhere), generally refers to these programs.

Although the large majority of persons involved in formal literacy training are enrolled in programs sponsored specifically by adult education legislation (and thus included in the statistics cited above), reading instruction is conducted through other channels as well. These include training programs administered through the federal government outside this legislation and programs conducted by a variety of other sponsors, including private industry, volunteer organizations, and individuals. Not only are persons who are taught through these programs not documented in the figures cited above, but, for a variety of reasons, they are also difficult to tabulate at all.

Many informal programs (such as the one conducted by the author for illiterate employees on a university campus) are not reported for any recordkeeping purpose. Various individuals and organizations are engaged in literacy training, using methods and materials provided by national literacy organizations, who no longer pay dues to these organizations and are not included in their statistics. Programs conducted by separate agencies within the government and within private industries are difficult to account for, both in terms of total enrollment figures and with respect to the extent to which many of these multifaceted programs are literacy oriented. Despite the impossibility of documenting the entire movement to cope with illiteracy, we will discuss several of its more significant aspects.

According to Peterson et al. (1979) some 600,000 in a total of approximately 2.8 million federal employees participated in 958,297 "instances" of training during the 1976 fiscal year. One percent of this training is classified as "basic literacy training." Although it is uncertain how many persons are involved, the 1 percent figure suggests that the number is significant.

Similarly, figures provided by Lusterman (1977) in *Education in Industry* (Conference Board report) indicate that roughly 1 percent of the training conducted in American industry is in basic literacy education. If Lusterman is correct that there are 5.8 million persons involved in industry training, 1 percent is no trivial total.

In addition to the government and industry programs which are involved in combating illiteracy, a number of volunteers are part of this effort. This volunteer movement received considerable impetus with the advent in

1971 of the National Reading Center (in conjunction with the beginnings of Right to Read), whose mission was to serve those who were either too young to be in school or youths and adults who were no longer associated with schools. As described by Stauffer (1973),

> The recognition of the massive manpower needs to teach literally millions of Americans led to the development of a plan for recruiting and training thousands of volunteer tutors. One of the stated basic functions of the Reading Center was to "promote volunteer tutoring programs that make use of the broad segment of citizenry and encourage peer group activity." [p. 256]

As Stauffer observes further, the use of nonpaid volunteers for teaching literacy was not new at this time. Dr. Frank C. Laubach's "Each One Teach One" campaigns had begun in 1931 and eventually spread to 105 countries. It was not until the mid-1950s, however, "that groups in the United States began to develop volunteer organizations that had as their exclusive concern the education of illiterate adults" (p. 256). As a consequence of this movement, the Texas Literacy Council, the first statewide literacy-oriented organization, was established in 1959. This was followed quickly by a number of additional councils, at least on the local level, throughout the country.

The volunteer effort is now a major part of the national effort to contend with illiteracy. A major portion of the volunteer movement is coordinated by two national literacy organizations: the National Affiliation for Literacy Advance and Literacy Volunteers of America, Inc., both headquartered in Syracuse, New York.

The National Affiliation for Literacy Advance (NALA), as the volunteer wing of Laubach Literacy International in North America, has trained and coordinates approximately 500 local literacy groups in about 40 states and Canada. In 1978, NALA had about 23,000 members who instructed over 27,000 students on a one-to-one basis. Since its establishment in 1968, NALA has also served as a forum for exchange of ideas between individuals and organizations involved in the literacy training effort and offers counsel and guidelines for the establishment and administration of volunteer literacy councils and projects.

Since its organization in 1962, Literacy Volunteers of America has taught over 40,000 persons to read, write, and speak English. In 1978, LVA affiliates were teaching in 83 communities in 20 states and 3 Canadian provinces. At present they tutor more than 10,000 adults on a one-to-one basis.

Additional literacy programs are administered and supervised by a variety of individuals and organizations. Literacy classes and one-to-one tutoring are conducted in many correctional facilities, both by volunteers and by local Adult Basic Education programs. A number of church groups also are involved in literacy work of one kind or another. These efforts are so diffuse as to be impossible to tabulate in any meaningful fashion.

In addition to funding provided through local Adult Basic Education programs, supported by the adult education legislation of the late 1960s and the 1970s, a number of programs that serve adult readers were funded through Right to Read under the U.S. Office of Education. According to information from OE, during the fiscal year 1978, funds totaling $5.3 million were made available for helping in- and out-of-school youths and adults through the Reading Academy Program (with emphasis on persons 17 years of age or older). In 1979 reading academies, which may be conducted through state and local education agencies, institutions of higher education, community organizations, and other nonprofit organizations, existed in 33 states, and providing reading assistance to approximately 15,000 youths and adults. Many of these academies employ methods and materials advocated by NALA or LVA.

The preceding information about various types of remedial programs is by no means exhaustive (nor could it be). Nonetheless, it provides some insight into the scope and variety of the literacy effort. A much more important undertaking is to estimate the outcomes of programs which constitute this effort.

## Remedial Education and Literacy Programs

For a variety of reasons, the impact of the various programs designed to combat functional illiteracy in the United States is extremely difficult to evaluate. Essentially, this is because accurate data are unavailable in many instances or are tabulated in a manner which is virtually impossible to interpret meaningfully. This section will focus upon Adult Basic Education programs derived from the adult education acts, since the most detailed information available pertains to this category of offerings.

Although a multitude of enrollment statistics exists with respect to programs which have stemmed directly from the adult education legislation of 1966 and 1969, these figures may be misleading. While there is no doubt that more educationally deficient adults are being served now, as a result of these programs, than a decade ago (3,371,265 documented participants in 1976 as opposed to 377,660 in 1966, as reported earlier), a number of problems arise which make it difficult to comprehend the impact of these data in functional literacy terms.

A first and obvious concern is what is meant by *enrollment*. Programs stemming from the adult education acts are required to report "enrollments" and these figures are lumped together to provide total tabulations of participants within each individual state and at the national level. In the final tabulations, however, it is difficult to determine just what "enrollment" means. Since local programs are under some compulsion to keep enrollment figures up in order to justify continued funding, it is likely that these figures often include persons who registered but dropped out after attending few, if any, classes (or independent study). Because attrition rates in Adult Basic Education programs are likely to be one-third or more of those initially enrolled (Coles, 1976) and because most dropouts occur during the first fifty hours of class attendance (Moss and Richardson, 1967), this possibility is not at all unlikely.

Another difficulty in interpreting the impact of Adult Basic Education programs on functional literacy is that no records are kept pertaining either to illiterates enrolled or new literates "created." Any effort to approximate these figures must be based upon grade-level standards which are at best only rough indicators of literacy level as discussed earlier. Furthermore, in terms of functional literacy, there is no way of determining what individuals can accomplish from examining data pertaining to their assigned grade levels.

A final obstacle in the effort to interpret state and national Adult Basic Education data in literacy terms is the fact that grade levels (misleading though they may be) are recorded only in groups. First, second, and third grades, for example, are often lumped together as a single category, so that there is no way of determining how many students are enrolled at a single grade level. If one were interested in approximating the number of persons in ABE classes who are total illiterates, for example, it is probable that he would be especially interested in knowing the number of students who are instructed at first grade level. Such information is generally unavailable as data are presently recorded.

The uncertain implications of state and national Adult Basic Education literacy statistics have not precluded efforts to draw inferences from these statistics, although in many cases these inferences may have little meaning. Consider the following excerpt from "The State of the Art of Reading in Virginia," a paper prepared as part of the Right-to-Read effort in Virginia:

> What of the adult population? Although precise data concerning the extent of illiteracy among adults in the state are not available, some inferences can be made. A report submitted by the Adult Education Service, State Department of Education, compared the educational attainment of the total population 25 years and older in 1960 with attainment a decade later in 1970. The percentage of the total population completing no schooling dropped from 2.7 percent in 1960 to 1.6 percent in 1970. The percentage of total population completing 1 to 4 years of schooling dropped from 10.5 percent in 1960 to 6.0 percent in 1970. It is estimated that one adult in every 20 may be a functional illiterate.
>
> A second report by the Adult Education Service dealt with enrollment of adults in reading skills courses by grade levels (grades 1-4 and 5-8) for a five-year period, 1971-75. The number of persons completing Level 1 (grades 1-4) increased from 1,170 in 1971 to 1,661 in 1975, and the number of persons completing Level 2 (grades 5-8) increased from 1,467 in 1971 to 4,191 in 1975. The

report stated that reading skills programs are a predominant element of the
adult basic education program for Level 1. Therefore, it can be assumed that
those persons who have completed this level may have learned to read for the
first time and have improved their reading skills by one or more grade levels.
[p. 5]

It is undoubtedly true that a number of persons have received instruction
helpful in addressing their literacy needs. The preceding excerpt, however,
may be misleading in its implication that substantial progress is being
made in the effort to contend with the illiteracy in Virginia. Although the
percentage of persons in the state with no schooling may have declined, it
is probable that the total number of functional illiterates actually has risen,
as it has in the nation during the same period. While the percentage of the
total population completing the early years of school increased during the
1960s, so did the demands for functional literacy, so that grade-level equiva-
lents associated with literacy are now higher than at any time in the past.
Furthermore, the emphasis upon the fact that many persons have improved
their reading skills by one or more grade levels suggests a misleading standard of measurement. The fact that an adult improves his reading by a
single grade level may be meaningless in the real world unless it translates
into functional reading competence.

As discussed earlier, grade levels and functional competencies do not
always correlate. Often a student who demonstrates considerable progress
in reading job orders or safety regulations (or other job- or life-related
materials) fails to demonstrate this progress on standardized tests. Similarly,
students who have been taught primarily with school and test-type
materials may fail to carry over their progress to "real life" reading matter.

We have suggested that the numbers of persons who appear in Adult
Basic Education enrollment tabulations might suggest inflated estimates
of those who actually are helped in functional literacy terms. It is interesting to note, however, that even the total numbers of persons served represent only a scant proportion of educationally deficient adults. Table 2 lists
the top areas in order of percentage of target population served. This
table, constructed from information provided by the National Advisory
Council for Adult Education, also includes for each area listed the size of
the target population (adults 16 years of age and over with less than a high
school diploma not currently required to be in school) and the size of the
Adult Basic Education enrollment. As table 2 clearly indicates, only a distinct minority of undereducated adults are reached by ABE programs,
even in those places where (in terms of numbers) Adult Basic Education is
the most effective.

Although the percentage of target audience served has increased stead-
ily since 1966, the National Advisory Council on Adult Education esti-

Table 2. Areas Ranked by Percentage of Target Populations Reached by ABE Programs (1976 Data)

| Rank | Area | Target Population | Enrollment | Percentage of Target Population Reached |
|------|------|-------------------|------------|------------------------------------------|
| 1 | California | 4,450,000 | 1,100,000 | 33 |
| 2 | Massachusetts | 1,415,564 | 250,000 | 18 |
| 3 | Hawaii | 456,000 | 56,589 | 12 |
| 4 | Florida | 2,333,000 | 265,625 | 16 |
| 5 | District of Columbia | 215,018 | 21,346 | 10 |
| 6 | Utah | 179,743 | 15,918 | 9 |
| 7 | South Carolina | 916,775 | 82,451 | 9 |
| 8 | Puerto Rico | 1,317,628 | 75,411 | 6 |
| 9 | Idaho | 164,279 | 7,813 | 5 |
| 10 | Maine | 245,000 | 24,700 | 5 |
| 11 | Nevada | 120,000 | 5,986 | 5 |
| 12 | North Carolina | 1,841,581 | 86,500 | 5 |

*Source:* Based upon the data in the *Annual Report* (National Advisory Council for Adult Education, 1977).

mates that only 4.25 percent of U.S. citizens with less than a high school diploma were involved in Adult Basic Education or Secondary Adult Education programs in 1976. As cited earlier, the final report of the Adult Performance Level Project (1977) suggests that one-fifth of the U.S. adult population has severe functional literacy handicaps. In any case, it is evident that a tremendous number of educationally deficient adults, for whatever reasons, are not served by existing programs.

In addition to appraising Adult Basic Education programs from the standpoint of the proportions of potential audiences served, it is necessary to take a more in-depth look at what these programs are able to accomplish for those who are enrolled. Although it is difficult to evaluate precisely what happens in terms of literacy or functional literacy, there is encouraging indirect evidence that progress has occurred. For 1976, for example, the National Advisory Council for Adult Education reports the following accomplishments of ABE participants:

18,983 participants removed from welfare rolls = savings to nation of
$35,156,516
Cost of 100 hours of instruction for 18,983 participants = $2,372,875
61,621 participants obtained jobs = $320,429,200 put back into economy
Cost of 100 hours of instruction for 61,621 participants = $7,702,625
11,628 participants received citizenship
31,267 participants received drivers' licenses
29,623 participants registered to vote for first time    [p. 21]

Although existing Adult Basic Education programs serve only a small percentage of undereducated persons, these statistics suggest that these programs have an impact in terms of increasing their participants' real-life coping skills. It is, of course, impossible to determine exactly what proportions of the accomplishments reflected above are directly attributable to ABE programs as opposed to other factors.

# Conclusion

This chapter has reviewed and analyzed the scope of illiteracy in the United States from a number of standpoints. Discussion has focused upon various means of defining this term, upon approximating the numbers of persons to whom it applies, according to different conceptualizations, and upon examining the cost of illiteracy in both human and economic terms. The last major section reviewed the various categories of programs designed to meet the needs of undereducated adults. Emphasis in this section has been upon programs which resulted as a direct consequence of the Adult Education Acts of 1966 and 1969, since these are the programs which serve the most people and upon which the most data are available.

The material in this chapter suggests that illiteracy in the United States remains a serious problem, despite the fact that society's effort to contend with it is more comprehensive than at any time in the past. In this context, it is important to keep in mind that even as programs grow and the number of minimally educated persons diminishes, the extent of functional literacy competence needed to cope with modern living continues to increase.

# Chapter 2

# The Adult Illiterate and the Environment

The adult learner differs from the preadult in a number of significant respects. In addition, the adult remedial reader is a rather unique species of adult learner whose environmental background often differs considerably from that of his teachers. The beginning of this chapter will focus upon the nature of the adult learner with respect to a number of separate but related dimensions pertaining to psychological and personality development, language factors, and needs and expectations of illiterates in formal learning situations. The latter portion of the chapter focuses upon general characteristics of the environments in which many adult illiterates live and work and how these factors may affect their classroom performances.

## Prior Learning

The learner always begins with his personal experience. As Frank Smith observes, "there must be a point of contact between what the student is expected to know and what he knows already" (1975, p. 9). Without this continuity, any new material is "nonsense" to a particular learner, "no matter how meaningful it may appear to anyone else."

The adult comes to a learning situation with a broad background of experience not possessed by the youthful learner. Simply through such

The coauthor of this chapter is Elizabeth B. Bolton.

commonplace daily activities as making a living and providing for a family, the adult acquires insights not easily discernible to a child. These activities allow him an understanding of relationships in the world around him. At the same time, through his unique experiences and life roles as worker, parent, and community member, he acquires social skills, language patterns, values, attitudes, and behaviors which may be difficult to change. As a consequence of this combination of circumstances, the adult's prior learning may be both an asset and a disadvantage to his efforts in the classroom.

From a motivation standpoint, the adult's background experience has enabled him to set his own priorities for learning. Unlike the child, who is in school because someone else has decided he belongs there, the adult seeks only those educational experiences he believes will improve the quality of his life. The adult's prior learning thus dictates and stimulates his learning objectives.

## Implications

The background experiences of functional illiterates may be both a help and a hindrance to their efforts to learn to read. Compared to the preadult beginning reader, the adult illiterate usually has a much more extensive speaking vocabulary. Furthermore, he is able to relate to many concepts, discussed in print, which are totally foreign to the child. The adult's motivation for reading is directed toward specific materials which are important in his personal life; thus he is apt to be more dedicated and industrious than his youthful counterpart, since he is in a position to make immediate application of what he learns.

In contrast to the preceding assets, with which the adult illiterate's prior learning may have equipped him, he is apt to suffer from an extremely negative view of himself as a learner. In remedial education for adults, perhaps the greatest obstacle represented by prior learning is a bad experience with formal schooling in childhood. As Landsman (1962) observes, a series of threatening or frightening school years promotes a feeling of self-worthlessness and continued avoidance of learning. Even for the adult illiterate who decides to venture again into the classroom, the recollection of failures may be a severe handicap. The slightest frustration may be interpreted by this student as confirmation of his prior learning *that he cannot learn to read.*

# Self-Concept

The self-concept of an individual is a very important factor in the way he approaches every aspect of life. The relevance of a positive self-concept to learning outcomes has been the subject of considerable research, most of which has dealt with youthful learners. According to Knowles (1970), however, "the single most critical difference between children and adults as learners is the difference in assumptions we make about their self-concepts" (p. 44).

The adult's self-concept has been evolving from the time of his birth. All individuals with whom he has had extended contact have in some way affected his perception of self. His life experiences have also contributed to the way he perceives himself.

The adult learner bases his idea of self on very different assumptions from those of a young learner. Knowles sees these differences as resulting from the adult learner and the young learner being at different points on a continuum that moves from dependency to autonomy. Children's self-concepts are at the dependency end of the continuum; the way they perceive themselves is totally dependent on their parents and the other individuals around them. The child's primary identity is that of a learner, but as the child matures, he moves closer to being a self-directed person. As the individual moves from dependency to autonomy, he begins to assume new roles in life, such as worker, spouse, and parent. The individual begins to feel more self-directed as he progresses along the continuum. He also has a need to feel that others view him as a self-directed person.

Given the need of the adult learner to view himself as self-directing, adult educators need to involve each student in taking responsibility for his own learning. Knowles makes a number of suggestions for planning adult education activities, from which can be derived the following guidelines.

1. Attention should be given to establishing a climate that is conducive to learning. This means that, in addition to a physical environment appropriate to adult learning needs, a psychological climate must be established that conveys acceptance, respect, and support. Knowles suggests that the behavior of the teacher is the most important factor in influencing the learning climate for adults.

2. Diagnosis of learning needs must be made with the active involvement of the learner. Knowles suggests a process of self-diagnosis, which consists of three steps: (a) constructing a model of what is desired or expected, (b) providing experiences which help the learner assess his present level of competence in view of the model, and (c) helping the learner measure the discrepancy between his present state and that which he wishes to achieve. This process identifies a need and provides a motivation to learn.

3. The adult learner must be involved in planning how he will meet the learning needs he has identified. This should be a mutual understanding between the teacher and the learner.

4. In conducting learning experiences, the teacher assumes the role of

a resource person or catalyst, not simply that of dispenser of information.

5.  The evaluation of learning is a joint endeavor between the teacher and the learner. The result is a rediagnosis of learning needs that sets the stage for future and perhaps advanced inquiry.

## Implications

Probably the most important aspect of the functional illiterate's self-concept in regard to formal learning situations was cited in the preceding section: his extreme lack of confidence in his ability to succeed. This difficulty not only magnifies frustration as the struggling nonreader tries to make sense of print, but increases dropout rates as well.

A related self-concept liability of the functional illiterate is his susceptibility to "field dependence," a problem which will be discussed at greater length in the section pertaining to social environment. Basically, this concept, as regards undereducated adults, has to do with the fact that a person with a low self-concept in a given situation (such as the adult illiterate's insecurity in the classroom) is more vulnerable to social pressure than a person with a higher self-concept. The adult illiterate's low academic self-concept thus makes him especially susceptible to social pressures in regard to his educational involvement. Often there is little encouragement in his living environment for educational pursuits, which may even bring him into disfavor with his peers.

Several cautions are in order in regard to the preceding guidelines for planning adult education activities. These guidelines are consistent with the organizational principles which are evident in successful adult learning programs. The problem is that adult remedial readers are often slow to accept these principles, since their past associations with school have involved them in little responsibility for planning their own learning.

Although the undereducated adult usually comes gradually to realize that he needs to take this responsibility, he may be reluctant to do so at first. The perceptive teacher should thus be careful to play (to an extent) the dominant role expected of him as he encourages the adult remedial reader to become more and more self-directing in planning and evaluating his learning activities. Otherwise, the insecure functional illiterate may become even more frustrated and intimidated.

## Aging and the Ability to Learn

An important factor which has discouraged adult participation in formal learning activities is the widespread belief that, as an adult advances in age, his ability to learn diminishes accordingly. This is perhaps the most subtle and damaging attitude with which educators must cope in working with adult learners.

Although some earlier research appeared to suggest that intellectual functioning declines with age, more recent studies imply that age alone is not a significant factor with regard to learning capacity. Some decline usually occurs in speed-oriented tests but not in untimed verbal tests, which are often better indicators of an individual's capacity to benefit from instruction. Furthermore, the vocabularies of most adults improve with age. This is significant in view of the fact that many psychologists have considered vocabulary the single most important measure of intelligence.

## Implications

Age alone need not discourage adult students or their teachers. We have worked successfully with persons who came to us as total nonreaders in their late sixties, and we are familiar with cases of students considerably older. In view of the fact that adult verbal abilities do not decline with age and vocabularies may actually improve, this seems hardly surprising.

Nonetheless, there are age-related considerations which perceptive teachers must keep continually in mind. Older students, of course, are much more apt to be handicapped by visual and hearing difficulties, which may interfere with instruction. When these persons are economically disadvantaged, as is frequently the case, they often have not had their vision or hearing checked on a regular basis. One of our students, a sixty-six-year-old lady, was wearing glasses which she had worn for ten years. When we set up an eye appointment for her, and she eventually received new glasses, both her performance and her morale improved dramatically.

Often, adult learners are embarrassed or otherwise reluctant to discuss their hearing and vision difficulties. One of our older students, for example, sat through an entire session, in which we made extensive use of a tape recorder, without telling us that she was unable to hear a word.

Because of the likelihood that older adults may have physical conditions which hinder their efforts in learning to read, it is especially important that the teacher be on the lookout for these difficulties and devise means of minimizing their effects. Although vision and hearing deficits are the most obvious such conditions, other factors bear watching as well. Older adults are more easily fatigued and are susceptible to various temporary ailments which may affect their concentration. In most cases, however, partial or temporary physical handicaps do not dictate that these persons cannot learn or should not be taught to read.

# Developmental Stages of Adulthood

Just as educators who work with youthful learners need to be aware of the latter's stages of development, educators who work with adult learners need an understanding of the stages of development experienced by adults at different points during the life span. Knox (1977) suggests that adult educators need to study adult development because: (1) It can be used to provide a better understanding of the holistic, comprehensive nature of an individual adult's life; (2) it provides an understanding of the sequential nature of the successive phases of adulthood; (3) it aids in understanding the transition from one phase of adult life to a later and successive phase; and (4) it enables individuals to gain greater insight and perspective into their own lives. Generally speaking, knowledge of adult development aids the adult educator in understanding the needs, interests, and motivations of particular clients and in planning and evaluating instructional activities.

The study of adult development raises questions related to the term itself. When does a person become an adult, and what is meant by development? The concept *adult* has been defined in terms of age, psychological maturity, and social roles. *Psychological maturity* is complicated and difficult to measure, while *age* tends to exclude individuals who should be included. As a result, social roles constitute perhaps the most meaningful criteria by which adulthood may be defined. Social roles include head of household, worker, parent, spouse, etc. Houle (1972) uses the social-role criteria and defines an adult as "a person who has achieved full physical development and who expects to have the right to participate as a responsible homemaker, worker, and member of society" (p. 229).

The concept of *development* has also been described in a number of ways. Hurlock (1975), for example, states that "the term *development* means a progressive series of changes that occur in an orderly and predictable pattern as a result of maturation and experience" (p. 12).

Various psychologists and researchers have conceptualized the stages of human life in somewhat different ways. Perhaps the best-known treatment is that of Erickson (1963, 1968), who presents a theoretical view of the human life cycle in eight stages, the first five of which are concerned with childhood and adolescence. Erickson looks at the various life stages on a continuum, and though his theory has not been tested empirically, it provides a sense of continuity in viewing the developmental process. His eight stages represent a series of crucial turning points. Starting with the beginning of life, these stages and their approximate durations are:

1. Trust vs. Mistrust          (0–2 years)
2. Autonomy vs. Shame          (2–4 years)
3. Initiative vs. Guilt        (4–6 years)
4. Industry vs. Inferiority    (6–12 years)
5. Identity vs. Confusion      (13–20 years)

6. Intimacy vs. Isolation     (20–30 years)
7. Generativity vs. Self-absorption   (30–50 years)
8. Integrity vs. Despair    (50 years–death)

The early stages or dilemmas to be resolved establish foundations or building blocks upon which success or failure at later points of development depends.

Since Erickson's early stages focus entirely on childhood and his last two stages encompass the entire latter half of life, his framework is rather vague as to the specific developmental issues of the middle and later years. Peck (1956) sees these periods more definitively and outlines what he considers to be their most important challenges. For middle age, he sees these as:

1. Valuing wisdom vs. valuing physical powers
2. Socializing vs. sexualizing human relationships
3. Cathectic flexibility vs. cathectic impoverishment (reactions to such events as death of parents, departure of children, etc.)
4. Mental flexibility vs. mental rigidity. [p. 25]

Peck identifies the three important issues in old age as:

1. Ego differentiation vs. work role preoccupation (adjustment to loss of occupation, etc.)
2. Body transcendence vs. body preoccupation
3. Ego transcendense vs. ego preoccupation.

Perhaps the developmental psychologist who has had the most influence on adult educators is Havighurst (1961), with his concept of *developmental task*, which he describes as follows:

A developmental task is a task which arises at or about a certain period in the life of the individual, successful achievement of which leads to his happiness and success with later tasks, while failure leads to unhappiness in the individual, disapproval by society, and difficulty with later tasks. [p. 2]

Examination of these tasks, as defined by Havighurst, reveals an implied sequential nature. For example, getting started in an occupation in early adulthood progresses to establishing and maintaining a standard of living in middle adulthood and, ultimately, to adjusting to retirement and reduced income in later maturity.

Developmental tasks in adulthood, of course, correspond to stages of life development. McCoy (1977) has presented a summary of developmental tasks that corresponds to the various stages of adult life, as reproduced in table 3.

## Implications

Although educators are well aware of developmental stages in the lives of children, this awareness is apt to be lacking in those who plan the

TABLE 3. ADULT DEVELOPMENTAL STAGES AND TASKS

| DEVELOPMENTAL STAGES | TASKS |
|---|---|
| Leaving home<br><br>18–22 | 1. Break psychological ties<br>2. Choose careers<br>3. Enter work<br>4. Handle peer relationships<br>5. Manage home<br>6. Manage time<br>7. Adjust to life on own<br>8. Problem solve<br>9. Manage stress accompanying change |
| Becoming Adult<br><br>23–28 | 1. Select mate<br>2. Settle in work, begin career ladder<br>3. Parent<br>4. Become involved in community<br>5. Consume wisely<br>6. Home own<br>7. Socially interact<br>8. Achieve autonomy<br>9. Problem solve<br>10. Manage stress accompanying change |
| Catch–30<br><br>29–34 | 1. Search for personal values<br>2. Reappraise relationships<br>3. Progress in career<br>4. Accept growing children<br>5. Put down roots, achieve "permanent" home<br>6. Problem solve<br>7. Manage stress accompanying change |
| Midlife reexamination<br><br>35–43 | 1. Search for meaning<br>2. Reassess marriage<br>3. Reexamine work<br>4. Relate to teenage children<br>5. Relate to aging parent<br>6. Reassess personal priorities and values<br>7. Adjust to single life<br>8. Problem solve<br>9. Manage stress accompanying change |
| Restabilization<br><br>44–55 | 1. Adjust to realities of work<br>2. Launch children<br>3. Adjust to empty nest<br>4. Become more deeply involved in social life<br>5. Participate actively in community concerns<br>6. Handle increased demands of older parents<br>7. Manage leisure time<br>8. Manage budget to support college-age children and ailing parents<br>9. Adjust to single state<br>10. Problem solve<br>11. Manage stress accompanying change |
| Preparation for retirement<br>56–64 | 1. Adjust to health problems<br>2. Deepen personal relations<br>3. Prepare for retirement<br>4. Expand avocational interests<br>5. Finance new leisure<br>6. Adjust to loss of mate<br>7. Problem solve<br>8. Manage stress accompanying change |

Table 3.    (Continued)

| Developmental Stages | Tasks |
| --- | --- |
| Retirement<br><br>65+ | 1. Disengage from paid work<br>2. Reassess finances<br>3. Be concerned with personal health care<br>4.˙ Search for new achievement outlets<br>5. Manage leisure time<br>6. Adjust to more constant marriage companion<br>7. Search for meaning<br>8. Adjust to single state<br>9. Be reconciled to death<br>10. Problem solve<br>11. Manage stress accompanying change |

Source: Vivian R. McCoy, "Adult Life Cycle Change," Lifelong Learning: The Adult Years (1977), 1 (2): 14–15.

learning activities for adults. It often appears that adults are viewed as having a straight-line existence from postadolescence to death. The fact is, of course, that an adult learner's position in life, where he is in his own personal development, has a tremendous impact on what he chooses to learn and how much he is able to profit from instruction. Each stage of adult development brings with it a unique set of preoccupations and tasks, which dominates the individual's orientation to learning. Learning activities which are consistent with the individual's preoccupations thus receive his undivided attention, while learning activities outside this range are apt to have little meaning.

Developmental tasks correspond to what Havighurst calls "teachable moments." Much of adult education revolves around the efforts of adult learners to contend with particular events and circumstances in their lives. An individual may be very interested in a course in prenatal care at one point in life and not at all at others. Similarly, persons in midlife much more readily attend a "Preparation for Retirement" seminar than persons just beginning their work careers.

What are the implications of all this for adult remedial readers? The acts of acknowledging one's illiteracy and one's need for help, then submitting to literacy instruction and its accompanying risks of failure and embarrassment, require considerable fortitude. Literacy and Adult Basic Education programs reach only a small proportion of undereducated adults. Many who enroll drop out as they determine that they are not making sufficient progress to justify continued effort and sacrifice. What factors, then, identify adult learners who enroll and persist in remedial reading programs? Why have they picked this point in their lives to try again to learn to read, despite the sacrifices required?

There is no single answer to this question. A variety of personality and environmental factors play a part, but a key factor is motivation—motivation which is inevitably related to the adult's developmental psychology.

Perhaps the desire to read is a general self-fulfillment issue, associated especially with a search for personal values for most persons during the thirties and forties or the postretirement years. Several of our older students, who focused their reading efforts primarily on the Bible, appeared to be in the latter category. Perhaps, as suggested earlier, the adult's intensified desire to learn to read stems from a more concrete work-related concern, involving, for example, a midlife promotion or change in occupation. In any case, it is apparent that his desire to learn *now*, to make sacrifices he has not made before, is related to his overall developmental process. He has arrived at a crossroads; his prior learning, self-concept, and total life circumstances have evolved to a point where learning to read has become a top priority.

The developmental tasks listed by McCoy do not necessarily apply to all individuals who are illiterate, especially those in the lower socioeconomic groups. The person who has not learned to read by his middle years is *perhaps* not primarily concerned (for example) with the need to "participate actively in community concerns" or to "manage [his] budget to support college-age children"—or other tasks which suggest an affluent and educated background. To date, there has been little research on the developmental tasks of the underprivileged and undereducated beyond descriptions of their basic survival needs, but the challenge to the educator is to discover what Havighurst calls the "teachable moment." An understanding of human development helps the teacher identify periods when the motivation to learn is present, which may stem from a particular stage of adult development or the passage from one stage to another.

# Personality and Language Factors

There are two additional areas of consideration for those who teach adult remedial readers: personality and language factors, which must be taken into account in planning instruction for these students.

## Personality Traits

In comparing the personalities of adult learners generally with those of children, Zahn (1967) describes the difference as follows: "They [adults] are more expressive, more expansive, and more outgoing. The high anxiety of youth is moderated by greater feelings of autonomy, of competence, and of stability. Adult moods are more even, as they have learned impulse control, and have a more unified identity" (p. 7). While this distinction may be generally valid in regard to adults and children as a whole, it presents an overly optimistic picture of the adult illiterate in the instructional setting. Undereducated adults in formal learning situations reflect the personality patterns that Zahn suggests are typical of children. In part, this is attributable to the functional illiterate's insecurity in the classroom and, in part, it results from a variety of social and economic conditions (discussed later).

Clearly, most teachers of undereducated adults appreciate the obvious virtues of these persons, including their earnest efforts to improve themselves. In their efforts to encourage students toward greater self-direction and learning independence, however, teachers must keep in mind some particular traits of adult remedial learners which may pose difficulties. Functional illiterates may be handicapped by a number of personality factors which can interfere with learning and discourage persistence.

Puder and Hand (1969) have stressed the tendency of the educationally disadvantaged individual to become close-minded, alienated, and passive in the face of life circumstances he feels powerless to control. They have further cited the inclination of the undereducated person toward avoidance of any stimulus he fears (including, of course, anything to do with school) and emphasized his tendencies of hostility and anxiety toward authority, withdrawal, shyness, feelings of disability, and lack of interest in overall intellectual development.

It must be emphasized that the characteristics described here are generalizations and are by no means descriptive of all adult illiterates. At the same time, however, teachers should be constantly aware that, whatever vulnerabilities students have in these areas, they are likely to be intensified by anxiety-provoking classroom situations.

## Language Handicaps

Language factors relating to functional illiterates will be discussed further in the section pertaining to social environment. At this point, it is sufficient to stress that language may be a problem for the functional illiterate for two reasons:

1. The discrepancy between the spoken language of the undereducated adult and the printed materials he aspires to read.
2. The discrepancy between the spoken language of the undereducated adult and that of his usually middle-class teacher.

While the functional illiterate's spoken language may be quite adequate for communicating with his peers, the teacher should be aware of potential language difficulties in the classroom situation. As will be discussed later, communication is often complicated by individual language idiosyncrasies, by interference from second-language patterns, or simply because of discrepancies between standard and nonstandard English dialects.

## Further Needs and Expectations

In addition to the general issues discussed in previous sections, the adult remedial reader brings a number of other needs and expectations to the classroom. For this discussion we have borrowed the following principles of adult learning cited by Gibb (1960):

1. Learning must be problem centered.
2. Learning must be experience centered.
3. Experience must be meaningful to the learner.
4. The learner must be free to look at the experience.
5. The goals must be set and the search organized by the learner.
6. The learner must have feedback about progress toward goals. [pp. 58–61]

In terms of the functional illiterate, these principles have clear implications for the planning of instruction and the selection of materials. The functional illiterate's primary need is not simply to "read reading" but to master particular printed messages with which he comes in contact in his daily living and working environments. As a result, his literacy training should focus upon his actual life needs. If he needs to be able to read job orders, for example, these need to be part of his curriculum, and he needs to be assured at least meager success with them from the beginning. Learning occurs in a personal and supportive atmosphere, where the learner is helped to set realistic levels of aspiration and may acquire continuous feedback, both from his instructor and from his own observations of progress. These basic guidelines will be referred to a number of times in our chapters on teaching strategies because we believe they are essential to any instructional program involving adult illiterates.

On the whole, although adult remedial readers face a number of formidable obstacles, most have the potential for significant learning success. For this potential to be realized, however, the perceptive teacher must carefully cultivate the adult learner's greatest asset—his motivation to learn. As James Dinnan (1971) puts it, the beginning adult remedial student will quickly develop one of two basic attitudes about his return to the classroom. His reaction will be either "the same old thing again" or "I'm certainly glad I gave it another chance" (p. 37). The possibility for the latter reaction can be maximized by reading programs which reduce the adult illiterate's anxiety and uncertainty while at the same time providing an instructional system compatible with his needs.

## Teaching Reading to Adults and Children

As might be inferred from the fact that we have addressed a lengthy discussion to the nature of the adult learner, we feel there are important differences in teaching adults to read as compared to teaching children. We must make it clear from the outset, however, that these differences do not suggest that adults and children differ in their basic learning processes. As we will discuss in more detail in the following section of this book, both groups, in our view, learn to read along the same general lines as they learned to speak. Both need continued exposure to a full context of written language as well as feedback concerning their efforts to interact with print.

Despite basic similarities in the manners in which adults and children process information, there are certain practical considerations pertaining to the teaching of illiterate adults which do not apply to children in the same degree. These relate to physiological differences, time constraints, previous experience, language differences, motivation, and learning expectations. Since these factors have been suggested by the material presented earlier in this chapter, and will be emphasized again in our instructional design, we will discuss each of them only briefly at this point in order to highlight some of the primary differences in the teaching (as opposed to the basic learning processes) of beginning adult readers and beginning child readers.

## Physiological Differences

Especially among older adults, the likelihood of hearing, visual, or health problems is increased. As discussed earlier, these conditions may affect both the adult's overall endurance in an instructional setting and his ability to respond effectively to certain types of activities (as in the case of the student who was bewildered by an entire lesson because of her inability to hear the tape recorder). Although teachers cannot eliminate all physiological problems which might handicap adult remedial readers, a great many of these problems can be neutralized or compensated. Perceptive teachers who are aware of particular physiological problems experienced by adult learners can often arrange learning activities in a manner which minimizes the impact of these difficulties, at least while the student is in the classroom. The point is that the teacher must be aware; he must not take for granted, as is usually the case with children, that the student has no physiological limitations.

## Time Constraints

In the case of the child, most of his time is spent in school—school consumes much of his life and thought. On the other hand, most adults have other, more pressing life concerns, revolving mostly around jobs and family. Relatively little time can be devoted to formal learning activities. In most instances, adult reading classes involve only a few hours each week of what otherwise would be leisure time which participants could devote to their families and friends. As a result, instruction must be carefully streamlined to provide as much immediate "payoff" and satisfaction as possible. It must focus on each individual's most important reading needs and on activities that are efficient in addressing them. Emphasis must be placed on practical materials (a newspaper ad, for instance, or a telephone book) which the adult perceives as relevant to his daily life and work. Activities must be so arranged as to guarantee the student some measure of immediate success, even if insignificant in real-life terms.

The part-time adult student does not have time for many units of study often presented to children. As a consequence, he will likely become impatient with such material as, for example, a unit on study skills, and perhaps choose to give up classroom instruction altogether.

## Previous Experience

As discussed at length in a previous section, adults have a great deal more breadth and depth of experience than children. In teaching children and adolescents, a great deal of time is devoted to building up their knowledge of the world — to increasing their background information in areas toward which their reading will be directed. In the adult's case, time constraints do not afford this opportunity, which is often unnecessary anyway. In the first place, the adult has a broader general background than the child. Furthermore, in the practically geared adult reading program, the student bears a primary responsibility for determining the materials upon which his instruction will focus. Generally, he selects printed matter directly relevant to his life and work — for which he already has considerable background and interest.

## Language Factors

As part of his broader, overall experience, the adult student is apt to have a more highly developed spoken language than the preadult learner. This is suggested not only by logic but by the fact that when beginning adult remedial readers are exposed to diagnostic tests designed for children (as is too frequently the case), they generally test at higher grade levels for vocabulary than in any other areas. Although we are not basically in sympathy with this sort of subtest assessment, this observation suggests that illiterate adults are apt to have more extensive vocabularies than children who are judged to be able to read at comparable levels. As a consequence, the teacher may not have to spend as much time on vocabulary directly, or in explaining concepts to which unfamiliar vocabulary relates, as would likely be the case with preadult learners.

## Motivation

As suggested in previous sections, adults and preadults usually have different motivations for learning to read. Adults want to learn to read (or increase their reading competence) as a means of improving the quality of their lives or, more specifically, to meet the literacy demands of their daily living and working environments. Children may desire to learn to read simply to be "grown up," or to please someone else, or because reading is a skill they admire in others. These varying objectives effect differences in how children and adults are taught, both in terms of reading materials and in regard to the type and extent of external motivation the teacher must provide.

## Expectations and Learning Self-Concept

Many children approach reading with every expectation of success. Their families and friends have learned to read, and they are excited at the prospect. As a consequence, they enter instruction confidently and enthusiastically. Although the first-grade teacher may have to temper the early expectations and disappointments of children who expected to learn to read the first day of school and *didn't*, he is dealing with basically confident learners. With most children this self-confidence is rewarded by fairly prompt success and visible progress. Only a few children who meet with continued frustration are apt to conclude that they cannot learn, and, of course, the more convinced they become of this, the more difficult they are to teach.

The teacher of adult functional illiterates must realize that virtually *all* his students are in the position of only a *few* children who have experienced extreme frustration. In fact, the emotional circumstances of most adult illiterates are worse. The adult has not only suffered longer, he has also paid a price for his inability to read.

This situation poses particular challenges for the teacher. The adult student must experience immediate success or he will drop out, confirming to himself his fears that he cannot learn. The teacher must organize instruction so that success (even if it is somewhat illusory) may be continually achieved. Also, the learner must always be in the position to tolerate and to learn from his mistakes, without being crippled by their effects. He requires steady support on a highly personal basis. These factors are, of course, important for children as well as adults, but their absence for adults with low learning self-concepts can easily destroy an adult remedial reading program.

## Social Environments of Adult Illiteracy

There can be no doubt that the various social environments in which an adult illiterate lives and works have a considerable impact upon his reading motivation and success. Nonetheless, it would be impossible to describe the social environments of illiteracy in a manner which is meaningful with respect to all adult remedial readers. There is no completely typical environment for illiteracy. Each illiterate comes from a unique combination of living, working, and peer group circumstances.

For several reasons, we will focus our discussion on the economically disadvantaged. Most, though by no means all, adult functional illiterates can be appropriately described in this manner. Furthermore, although the economically disadvantaged are a difficult group to recruit into adult basic and other remedial education programs, they are probably more apt to participate than persons with greater financial resources. The latter group not only has the means to employ private tutors but a greater potential for public embarrassment. Since this book is aimed primarily at teachers who address adult remedial readers in group settings, it is appropriate to focus on the disadvantaged as the group most likely to populate ABE classes.

Focus on the social environments of the disadvantaged is appropriate for another reason. Since most Adult Basic Education and remedial reading teachers are products of middle-class backgrounds, there are inevitably differences in the social support systems, living conditions, and values of these teachers as compared with their culturally and economically disadvantaged students. In cases where illiterate adults come from more privileged circumstances, teachers and students may be products of similar backgrounds. Under such conditions, they may already have the basis for an effective working relationship.

Our purpose in this section is not to present a comprehensive picture of the social environments of the disadvantaged. Such an undertaking would be neither practical nor relevant to our purposes. We will attempt, instead, to highlight some of the major areas where probable differences in the backgrounds of ABE (and other remedial reading) teachers and their disadvantaged students may hinder classroom communication. If teachers become more aware and more sensitive to these issues, the potential for a meaningful dialogue with their students will be increased.

Our initial treatment of the social environments of illiteracy will be divided according to four topical headings: family-related factors, work environment and peer group factors, language-related factors, and additional factors associated with poverty. These discussions are followed by a section which pertains to the purposefulness of the disadvantaged.

Before we embark on these topics, several cautions are in order. The following discussions make no pretense of analyzing and comparing individual minority cultures, such as those of the black inner-city ghetto or the white Appalachian rural poor, which differ from a sociological standpoint in any number of ways. What is offered here is a series of observations which, we believe, are applicable in varying degrees to adult remedial learners with a variety of disadvantaged backgrounds. It must be stressed that the generalities in which we will be speaking do not necessarily apply totally (or even partially) to all adult functional illiterates. Some of these persons may come from more affluent and educated backgrounds than those we describe. Others may not have been affected by their low socioeconomic status to the extent which we suggest is typical of their peers.

## Family-related Factors

It is likely that the teacher of undereducated adults comes from a family which encourages educational pursuits. Not only in most middle-class families is education valued for its own sake, but learning activities are supported in a number of ways. Homes are well endowed with books, newspapers, and magazines, which family members read regularly. Usually there is a relatively quite place to which the individual who wants to read or study can retire and concentrate. Most important, family members are encouraged in their learning endeavors. Middle-class adults who decide to take courses, or engage in formal educational activities of any sort, are usually applauded by their relatives.

The picture presented above is in sharp contrast to the family situation of the typical disadvantaged adult. Not only is the physical environment of his home not conducive to his school work, but also his educational involvement may have put a strain on the family. The homes of many disadvantaged persons are apt to be extremely crowded and noisy. There is little opportunity for concentration on school-related matters. Furthermore, it is likely that no one studies or reads and that little or no reading matter is available. There frequently are no educational models to encourage the functionally illiterate adult student.

In contrast to the encouragement offered by middle-class families for educational interests, disadvantaged families may resent the use of time for this purpose or the potential impact of the educational achievement of one family member on the family's accustomed interdependence patterns. The authors are reminded in this connection of the experience of a friend who taught a class for a number of functionally illiterate women employees in a university setting. These women studied for, and eventually passed, their drivers' license examinations. This achievement caused considerable dissension within the families of the students whose husbands feared a loss in their wives' dependence on them.

Deeply immersed in a lifestyle which focuses on the immediate present and emphasizes day-to-day existence, disadvantaged families seldom identify with the middle-class idea that one "gets ahead" through education. Present needs are simply too pressing to focus on delayed gratification. The attitude of the family toward a member who attends a class is likely to be something like "Why are you wasting time going to school when you ought to be taking care of us?"

Few adult remedial students, many of whom are apt to feel insecure in their educational involvement, can persist for long in the face of strong, domestic opposition. Although it has been observed by teachers that adult students who enroll and persist in remedial classes often have unusually strong family backing, many illiterates lack this support.

## Work- and Peer Group-related Factors

Educationally disadvantaged persons who are also employed are apt to be engaged in jobs which are physically demanding. If they choose to attend adult education classes, they must usually do so in the evenings, after a hard day's work which may leave them exhausted and thus detract from their ability to focus upon their reading or other classroom activities.

Frequently, the employment of functional illiterates is insecure. They are the group hardest hit by automation, in an age when one machine can replace hundreds of workers. Since they realize that they are the last hired and the first fired, disadvantaged adult students may be disturbed by this fact, to the point of losing concentration on educational matters. When the functional illiterate is unemployed, as is often the case, the situation is worse. London, Wenkert, and Hagstrom (1963) found that unemployed workers had the lowest adult education participation rate, despite their greater free time.

> It appears that unemployment often leads to a psychological sense of hopelessness, combined with apparent apathy and a virtual inability to exert energy and effort to improve one's position. This is probably most true when retraining does not insure subsequent employment. Before we can reasonably induce workers to enter the various manpower retraining programs around the country, we must make a greater effort to insure that the training is tied to jobs actually available in the labor market. Unless the result of retraining is the assurance of a definite job, we will only increase frustration and discontent among workers who are being replaced by machines and who may well constitute a permanent unemployed group in our society. [p. 150]

London, Wenkert, and Hagstrom follow these observations with the suggestion that employers institute programs of "day release" time that provide education and training as a condition for employment.

It is certainly true that work-release programs have been found to work effectively in a number of instances and that they usually suffer much lower attrition rates than part-time programs conducted by public schools or other public or private agencies. Nonetheless, participants in work-release training programs, especially those involving remedial education, are prone to suffer a unique difficulty within the work environment. Since attendance in remedial classes causes participants to miss time from their jobs, the employees who do not attend classes have more work to do. As a result, resentment and conflict often develop within the work environment. This may be true even though work-release participants have employer sanction to attend classes and complaining employees may have declined the opportunity themselves.

Despite a few effective work-release programs and occasional employer incentives for workers to participate in outside educational programs, the work environments of functional illiterates do not often provide encouragement for educational pursuits, which is often observed in middle-class work environments. In many cases, employers prefer that their lower-level workers remain at low educational levels, feeling that they will be less restless about changing jobs or struggling for promotion. As for the workers themselves, as long as they remain trapped in their lifestyle of day-to-day economic survival, they are unable to focus on delayed gratification, which might come from the effort to better themselves educationally.

Researchers have often found — as in a study by Prins (1972), for example — that Adult Basic Education dropouts blame conflicting commitments. Findings of this sort have puzzled teachers, who have observed that students who persist often have equally demanding pressures and responsibilities. London, Wenkert, and Hagstrom challenge the assertion that time pressures, per se, are a main factor in causing Adult Basic Education attrition (assuming that most ABE students are blue-collar workers, if they are employed at all). Rather, they find that:

1. Adult education participation is generally less among blue-collar workers than among white-collar workers.
2. The availability of leisure time is increasing for all workers.
3. The availability of leisure time is growing for all workers, but is growing faster among blue-collar than among white-collar workers.
4. People are most apt to participate in adult education activities if their friends participate (regardless of social level).
5. Blue-collar workers are no more than half as apt to have participant friends as white-collar workers.

These conclusions emphasize the importance of support from one's peer group and/or work associates for involvement in education. Regardless of the amount of leisure time available, most persons don't participate in educational activities unless their friends and associates do likewise. In the case of functional illiterates and other adult remedial learners, there is usually little sentiment among friends and fellow workers for educational pursuits.

## Language-related Factors

Bowren and Zintz (1977) call attention to a number of language difficulties confronted by the undereducated adult which may hinder his efforts to learn to read and his participation in educational activities generally. These include discrepancies between standard and nonstandard English, dialects, individual idiosyncratic language patterns, and inteference from patterns of a second language.

The key word in the preceding is *discrepancies*. The point is not that undereducated adults are incapable of communicating effectively; their styles of oral expression are often more than adequate for communicating *within* their social environments. Problems often arise, however, when the undereducated adult meets the middle-class teacher in an educational setting. A communication gap is apt to occur simply because of language differences in the speech patterns of teacher and student. Furthermore, the student is often asked to focus his reading efforts on content, vocabulary, and syntax, which are far removed from his background experiences.

While the difficulties described above are better conceptualized as language differences than as learner deficiencies, they represent problems for the undereducated adult in the teaching-learning situation. Not only do these factors hinder teacher-student communication, they often prevent accurate measurement of student learning potential.

If the student speaks only broken English, or a dialect which is different from his teacher's, it is apparent that a communication problem exists. Often, however, the problem is much more subtle and less easily detectable. Even where the teacher and the student speak ostensibly the same language and are able to understand each other in simple, informal conversations, communication difficulties are apt to occur in the classroom. Most teachers have been educated, and continue to live and work, in highly verbal environments in which they constantly process large amounts of spoken language, involving complex vocabulary and syntax and heavily laden with concepts. The undereducated adult may easily become lost and confused in a maze of verbiage which his teacher regards as direct and commonplace.

Although the functional illiterate may have a broad background of experience (more, in some areas, than his teacher), it is often not the sort of experience that is easily related to classroom language patterns. Having been shut off from reading and other school-related activities in the past, the undereducated adult student is usually unaccustomed to abstract thinking and to many experiences typical of many middle-class adults.

The adult remedial learner may also be easily overwhelmed by vocabulary and syntax. Although his broader background and exposure to spoken language may give him some advantage over the child who is learning to read, he is not on a par with his teacher in this regard. He simply is not apt to live in an environment that emphasizes verbal communication in the manner that his instructor's does. Orem describes the speech of the "lower class" as follows:

> Their vocabulary is restricted, imprecise, and reflects a low level of conceptualization. Sentences tend to be short or incomplete, and syntactically simple; they often take the form of shouted commands, accompanied by grunts and gestures. As a rule, lower class parents do not talk over, at length with the child, what has happened, is happening, or could probably happen. [p. 103]

This characterization does not, however, apply to all adult illiterates.

Several studies have found that persons in lower socioeconomic class are "relatively nonintrospective" in their talk. According to Gordon (1968),

> their referents are largely external, concretistic events with internal events represented by the externals assumed but unverbalized. A young male client with whom I worked typified this; he would describe an experience he had had and in response to my probe about how he felt about the event, would, with some astonishment, describe the objective events again. He seemed to be saying, "Why, I feel like you feel when that happens to you. . . ." Thus, the lower class child grows up without attention to internal states, and therefore without a vocabulary for labeling that which he has not learned to discriminate. [p. 127]

Bernstein (1964) describes the lower class (not synonymous with "adult illiterate") as poor not only in words to describe feelings but in qualifiers, adjectives, and adverbs. This observation not only has implications for potential communication difficulties between teacher and student but may contribute to the problem of adult remedial readers who must often focus on printed language patterns which do not correspond to those of their own speech.

In addition to background factors, which are apt to place the adult remedial learner at a disadvantage in classroom communications, is the undereducated adult's reluctance to use his oral language in a situation where he feels insecure. Frequently, the fact that the adult student chooses to say as little as possible to his middle-class teacher in the classroom situation creates an unrealistically low impression of his language and mental abilities. Gordon illustrates this point from his experience with low-level socioeconomic blacks:

> There is a good deal of evidence indicating that, in social interactions with representatives of the large culture (i.e., "the man"), minority group members tend to become verbally inhibited. Thus, they speak less in structured situations

such as employment and counseling interviews, and in individual test sessions (therefore achieving lower IQ scores). I observed a dramatic instance of this reaction when visiting a group of Negroes living in a small "tent city" in rural Alabama. They had been evicted from their plantation shacks for having registered to vote. I was introduced to some of the tent city by a Negro worker who, in a sense, transferred his rapport with the residents to those of us accompanying him. Our conversation was quite animated and showed no dearth of expressive verbal activity on the part of the residents, until we were intruded upon by a strange white man taking movies of the tents. He was a local resident who revealed stereotyped segregationist and paternalistic sentiments. During the period of his participation in the group conversation, the Negroes spoke very little, assumed a passive expression, and gave monosyllabic answers. They stared off blankly into space, and looked "dumb" and uncomprehending, which attitude completely disappeared with the departure of the intruder.    [p. 125]

A final point about the language of the disadvantaged deserves discussion. Teachers may often be frustrated by an apparent inconsistency between the words and actions of the disadvantaged adult learner, or even inconsistency in his statements from one class meeting to the next. These tendencies may be attributable to a combination of a number of factors (which will not be discussed here in detail). Our purpose is simply to alert the teacher to the fact that such inconsistencies can be anticipated, to some extent, and don't necessarily reflect on the integrity of students.

It is apparent that some inconsistency between student talk and action is due to the disadvantaged adult's inclination to follow the path of least resistance by telling the teacher what he thinks the teacher wants to hear. On other occasions, such inconsistency may reflect unrealistic ambitions, especially of the young adult learner, which are beyond his potential for accomplishment. Overall, perhaps the biggest factor in the undereducated adult's frequent failure to associate words and actions (or statements with previous statements) has to do with the time perspective in which he lives. For the most part, his life is focused upon the immediate present, with little concern for where it "fits" in the continuity between past and future. Thus he is likely to lose sight of (or interest in) the relationship between his present words or actions and his past pronouncements.

If the Adult Basic Education and/or remedial reading teacher is to help his students, he needs to be aware of their language patterns and uses and, particularly, how these may differ from his own.

## Additional Factors Associated with Poverty

Certainly, for persons who are poor, most aspects of their lives are poverty related, and this obviously applies to the considerations discussed earlier, relating to home and work environments and to language factors. This section presents additional socioeconomic issues which are likely to have an impact on teaching-learning situations involving the educationally disadvantaged.

A major problem of the poor and undereducated, which is relevant for classroom situations, is health conditions. These segments of the population are disproportionately high in both number and severity of health problems. They are often uninformed about how to care for their health and unable to afford proper preventative medicine and dentistry. As a consequence, potentially controllable health conditions are ignored, eventually ladening the poor with heavier financial burdens than they are able to bear. The poor and undereducated are also ignorant of nutrition and unskilled at acquiring the necessary foods to balance diets within their limited budgets.

The health and other potential problems of functional illiterates should certainly be within the teacher's scope of awareness. Not only are students likely to be irregular in attendance because of health conditions, relating either to themselves or to members of their families, but their alertness may be impaired while they are attempting to learn.

The lower class of society, including most educationally disadvantaged adults, also differs from the middle class in a number of attitudinal respects. Although perhaps not all the listed comparisons relate specifically to teaching and learning in the remedial classroom, the difference in values (the "cultural chasm") between these two socioeconomic levels is described by Segelman (1965) and reproduced in table 4. When confronted with a total life situation which necessitates that life be oriented from paycheck to paycheck and often, literally, from hand to mouth, there is little opportunity for the individual to focus on the prospect of delayed gratification. This circumstance is particularly apparent from the lower-class attitudes toward education, money, and the future described in table 4. It is also apparent that functionally illiterate adults are apt to be indifferent, perhaps even belligerent, toward many middle-class values and distrustful of their teachers and the values they represent.

Of the considerable number of social factors which hinder the progress and persistence of nonreaders and other adult remedial students, environmentally engendered attitudes toward education, especially for adults, are among the most critical. To communicate with his students, the teacher must be aware of the extent to which these attitudes differ from those which predominate in his own middle-class culture.

# The Disadvantaged Not All Alike

The poor represent a substantial portion of the population. According to figures based on the Consumer Price Index, almost 15 percent of the

TABLE 4. THE CULTURAL CHASM

| THE CONCEPT OF ... | IN MIDDLE-CLASS TERMS STANDS FOR ... | BUT TO THE LOWER CLASS IS ... |
|---|---|---|
| Authority (courts, police, school principal) | Security — to be taken for granted, wooed | Something hated, to be avoided |
| Education | The road to better things for one's children and oneself | An obstacle course to be surmounted until the children can go to work |
| Joining a church | A step necessary for social acceptance | An emotional release |
| Ideal goal | Money, property, to be accepted by the successful | "Coolness": to "make out" without attracting attention of the authorities |
| Society | The pattern one conforms to in the interests of security and being "popular" | "The Man" — an enemy to be resisted and suspected |
| Delinquency | An evil originating outside the middle-class home | One of life's inevitable events, to be ignored unless the police get into the act |
| Future | A rosy horizon | Nonexistent; so live each moment fully |
| "The street" | A path for the auto | A meeting place — escape from a crowded home |
| Liquor | Sociability, cocktail parties | A means to welcome oblivion |
| Violence | The last resort of authorities for protecting the law-abiding | A tool for living and getting on |
| Sex | An adventure and a binding force for the family, creating problems of birth control | One of life's few free pleasures |
| Money | A resource to be cautiously spent and saved for the future | Something to be used now, before it disappears |

*Source:* Ralph Segelman, "The Cultural Chasm," Rocky Mountain Science Association (Spring, 1965); reprinted in Reba S. Mosby, *Challenge to Society: The Education of the Culturally Disadvantaged Child.* A Seminar for Teachers of the Culturally Disadvantaged, v.3 (New York: Pageant, 1971).

population of the South and 7 to 8 percent of the populations of other regions were below the poverty line ($5,050 for a nonfarm family of four, $4,300 for a farm family) in 1975. This category of persons has evoked a number of rather deficit-oriented statements in the literature, such as the following cited by Wilson (1975):

> The disadvantaged have the lowest income, the poorest education, the largest families, the highest incidence of ill health, the least chance of employment and little promise of a better future. In addition, the disadvantaged are hampered by certain psychological disabilities, including a lack of self-confidence, low self-esteem and a high degree of dependency. Because of their limited perception of the value of education, the disadvantaged display neither aspiration, nor motivation to achieve educational goals. Their lack of verbal facility impedes communication with other than their own kind. Consequently, they become outcasts, withdrawing further into their own sub-cultural milieus. In time, the relationship between the disadvantaged and others becomes increasingly tenuous so that the possibilities of communication are lessened and the opportunity for community involvement becomes minimal.    [p. 5]

Nonetheless, it is apparent that not all of the disadvantaged are incompetent or lacking in direction. Like any other segment of the population, some are, some aren't.

The poor have been subcategorized in various ways by different authors. One broad typology, emphasizing the attributes as well as the deficits of four groups of the disadvantaged, is that proposed by S. M. Miller (1964), which may be summarized as:

| | |
|---|---|
| The Stable Poor | This group includes the regularly employed, low-skilled families characterized by stability — economically and familially. |
| The Strained | This group reflects a secure economic pattern but an unstable family pattern. |
| The Copers | This group is composed of individuals and groups of individuals who show family stability but economic insecurity. These persons manage to keep themselves pretty well intact, even in the face of rough going economically. |
| The Unstable | This group has neither economic nor family stability. It is characterized by unskilled and irregular workers, large and broken families, and disproportionately higher numbers of physically handicapped and mentally disturbed. |

Although any such organization of categories is somewhat arbitrary, this breakdown suggests that an overall perception of the disadvantaged which focuses entirely on deficits is shortsighted and misleading. Although the poor may have different lifestyles, different values, and speak a different language than their middle-class counterparts, they are often quite capable and successful within their own perspectives. Also, many disadvantaged persons may be better candidates for adult education than we are inclined to believe. While research pertaining to the purposefulness of the disadvantaged is scanty at best, a few studies seem to support this conclusion. We will discuss briefly several of these undertakings.

A recent HEW-funded study, conducted by Hampton and Ashton (1979), addresses the perceived educational and training needs of the urban disadvantaged. The researchers acquired 120 usable interviews from 312 randomly selected households in a "homogeneous" 45-block area of about 6,000 residents in Savannah, Georgia. In this study (among other findings), 61 percent of respondents between 16 and 44 years of age and 48 percent of those over 45 years of age expressed the desire for some form of training. Close to a third of all respondents indicated that they wanted "basic training," a term not defined by the authors but usually construed to include basic literacy skills.

In a different research approach, Frandson (1970) compared the support for adult education participation he found at different socioeconomic levels. He hypothesized that variations in enrollment among different socioeconomic statuses are partly attributable to differences in the support, or lack of support, which adult education participants feel they receive from particular reference groups.

As reference groups, Frandson selected (1) family, (2) friends, and (3) admired people. He devised a questionnaire which examined 205 Los Angeles County adult students at different socioeconomic levels, according to three dimensions for each subject: (1) the support he received from each of the three potential reference groups, (2) the degree of equivalence between the individual's adult education norms and values and those of these groups, and (3) other aspects of the relationship between the student and his potential reference groups.

Frandson had expected to find that support system strengths differ appreciably among different socioeconomic statuses. Surprisingly, however, he found no significant differences, thus failing to support his original hypothesis and bringing him to the conclusion that socioeconomic status does not affect level of support for adult education activities.

The results of the Frandson study appear to conflict with those of earlier research and with the implications of the bulk of literature pertaining to the disadvantaged. While there is no obvious explanation for this apparent discrepancy, it may suggest either that the view of the disadvantaged toward education is less negative than previously apprehended or that this attitude is, in fact, growing more positive.

Another study, Kerckhoff and Campbell (1977), focused upon the value of socioeconomic status in predicting the academic success of school children. The status was found to be of questionable predictive value — much more effective, on the whole, for whites than for blacks.

# Implications

Despite this group of research studies, it is apparent that the environmental backgrounds of many ABE students place them at considerable disadvantage in any formal classroom situation. It is important, however, that this handicap, or teachers' attitudes toward this handicap, not be allowed to assure that adult illiterates remain second-class citizens. With its emphasis on survival skills, the present application of competency-based education in ABE is, in some respects, having that effect.

Competency-based education is in theory an appropriate approach to most adult education programming. In Adult Basic Education, however, this movement has become linked with an emphasis on teaching the individual the functional coping skills that he needs to survive in modern society. A frequent tendency of adult educators is to focus upon minor skills which are easily teachable. The result is that many "legitimate" adult reading goals are often neglected, including, for example, reading for working, for parenting, for buying, for government and law, or simply for pleasure. It is both erroneous and unfair to assume that students from disadvantaged backgrounds are capable and deserving of learning only "survival" skills. To quote Rosemarie Park (1979), "Teaching 52 adults 'how to make change' will not solve the literacy problem" (p. 1).

# Conclusion

We have attempted in this chapter to focus upon selected aspects of the nature of economically and educationally disadvantaged ABE students and the social environments in which they live and work. Our intent has *not* been to present an in-depth analysis of these issues; admittedly, we have barely scratched the surface. What we have hoped to do instead is to sensitize predominantly middle-class teachers to characteristics of the undereducated and the living and working conditions which are most likely to affect their motivation and performance in the ABE or remedial reading classroom.

Inevitably, at some points, our discussion has focused upon the apparent handicaps of predominantly poor ABE students in formal learning situations. It is dangerous and misleading, however, as we indicate, to view the disadvantaged entirely from a deficit perspective. Although supporting research is limited at best, there are indications that many disadvantaged persons are more purposeful than much of the earlier deficit-oriented literature suggested. Furthermore, reference-group support for adult education participation may be present among the lower socioeconomic group to a greater extent than previously realized.

Despite these somewhat encouraging insights, however, continued motivation and environmental support cannot be taken for granted for most ABE students. For remedial reading and other Adult Basic Education programs to have a successful impact, close attention must be focused on what Darkenwald (1974) has described as the "cultural dialogue" between teacher and student. Darkenwald found, for example, that black students tended to have lower dropout and absentee rates when taught by black teachers. It is hardly surprising that Adult Basic Education students, like other persons, draw their particular values and aspirations from the various social environments of which they are part.

Certainly, it is not often possible to match teacher and student according to cultural background. Failing this, however, it is important to do the next best thing: help teachers become aware of the differences between their backgrounds and those of their students, especially in regard to education values and support systems. It seems logical that students are more likely to persist and to learn in educational programs where their teachers are culturally equipped to understand their particular environmental problems and coping strategies.

# Part 2

# A Program of Reading Instruction

# Chapter 3

# The Reading Process

Since this is a book about the teaching of reading, it is appropriate to emphasize the nature of the reading process. It would be helpful at this point if we could present a single, integrated description of this process as experts view it. Unfortunately, there is little consensus on exactly what reading involves.

It is apparent that the more one studies the process of reading, the more he studies the processes of thinking and learning. Of all the complicated definitions of reading which have been offered by scholars, perhaps the safest (yet most convincing to us) is that of Farr (1977): "Reading is thought guided by symbols." This brief definition, of course, offers no implications about how the teaching of reading should be undertaken at various levels of learner independence, a task we shall attempt later. It does emphasize, however, perhaps the only points of definition upon which theorists agree. The fact that learning inevitably involves symbolic transfer of one sort or another, as well as the thinking process, may be the reason why reading and learning have always been closely related.

The difficulties in defining reading make it easier to understand why controversy exists over how the reading process works and how the fluent reader reads. Nonetheless, it is essential that the teacher work from a definite viewpoint of what he thinks reading is (though this may differ somewhat, depending on different students needs and their different degrees of independence) and of how he believes the fluent reader processes printed symbols. Only in this manner is the teacher in a position to set forth and defend his views of what the novice reader must learn in order to derive meaning from print. This is the only way in which the teacher can develop an integrated instructional program which continuously approaches the teaching of reading in a manner consistent with his view of how reading is learned. Otherwise, instruction tends to be capricious and often self-defeating; not only is the emphasis on teaching rather than learning, but some "lessons" may be unnecessary or suffer from a number of potential liabilities. They may negate each other's effects, complicate the abstraction of the reading process unnecessarily, or simply lower student morale, to no constructive purpose. These difficulties will be discussed in later chapters.

# Three Approaches

As a means of illustrating the complexity of the reading process and the diversity of ways in which it can be viewed, we will discuss three alternative conceptualizations: reading as a linear skill-building–thinking process, reading as a vision-thinking process, and reading as a language-thinking process. While there is some commonality in these three conceptualizations (as there is in most descriptions of reading), there are enough different points of emphasis to demonstrate the extent to which theorists differ. It must be stressed, of course, that while the three views of reading discussed here are sufficient to illustrate the diversity of views in the field, they are in a sense rather arbitrary choices. There are any number of ways in which the reading process has been labeled and conceptualized. Several of these are thoroughly reviewed by George and Evelyn Spache in the first chapter of their 1977 textbook *Reading in the Elementary School*. We recommend this book as an excellent reference for persons interested in alternative views of the reading process.

In addition to emphasizing the diversity of viewpoints about how reading "works," our primary purpose in discussing the three views we have chosen is to emphasize that one's beliefs about the nature of reading (even if such beliefs are below the level of conscious awareness) dictate the manner in which one teaches it. As will become apparent, we believe that a language-thinking or psycholinguistic view of the reading process is most consistent with existing evidence of how fluent readers process print. Our views of how reading is learned and how it should be taught (discussed in later chapters) are consistent with this conceptualization.

## Reading as a Linear Skill-Building–Thinking Process

This view of the reading process holds that the reader reacts separately to each word on the printed page in linear fashion, bringing to bear, in each case, "a group of mental associations regarding the word form, its meaning, and its sound" (Spache and Spache, 1977, p. 4). Thus this conceptualization begins with word recognition and suggests that the reader "holds in mind the meanings of the first words of the sentence as he reads those that follow. Similarly, the more mature reader retains the ideas of successive sentences" (Spache, p. 5).

At most, adherents to the skill-building view of reading focus only very limited attention on what the fluent reader does in processing print. They devote their primary emphasis instead to the effort to identify a supposed hierarchy of skills by which reading is most easily learned and therefore should be taught. The skill-building viewpoint implies that the beginner learns in a building block fashion, where he masters one skill, refines it, then repeats the cycle with a higher-level skill until reading fluency is achieved.

The skill-development view of reading is widely reflected in teaching practice for adults and children. Nonetheless, the idea that meaning is acquired from print in a straightforward additive and linear fashion, whereby the reader merely stores and combines the meanings of successive words and sentences, is drastically oversimplified. Skills are not learned or employed individually but in combination. Furthermore, although most basal series and other published programs for the teaching of reading would suggest otherwise, it has yet to be determined (except in the broadest terms) exactly what specific skills are involved in reading, much less in what order these skills must be acquired. This makes it especially distressing to observe reading-instructional programs in both adult literacy training and many public schools, where more attention is devoted to refining specific skills (by means of particular phonics drills, for example) than to allowing beginning and remedial readers to experience print in its full context.

When the novice reader is forced to focus extensively on word-attack skills before he has an overall sense of what reading is, he is not adequately equipped to grasp where the pieces fit in the puzzle. He is unable, in effect, to relate these skills meaningfully to the reading task because he doesn't fully comprehend what that task is. The adult illiterate, who often lacks confidence in his ability to read in the first place, needs to experience immediate success in his reading efforts and to be continuously aware of the relevance and purpose of the skills he is asked to refine. Otherwise, he not only may be hindered in his learning but also may become discouraged and discontinue his efforts.

The preceding remarks should not be taken to mean that we see no value in skill practice at any point in the learning-to-read process. We simply believe that skill building may easily become a clear case of the cart pulling the horse. Any person who struggles to derive meaning from abstract printed symbols is confronted with a task which is quite demanding, especially if it is one he has never before attempted or at which he has never experienced success. This abstraction is compounded by an instructional program which focuses on the mastery of intricate components of fragmented written language before it allows the student to increase his understanding of reading by a holistic exposure to print in full sentences of natural syntax. This emphasis on full context for beginning readers may be accomplished through a variety of strategies to be discussed in later chapters, including language experience, assisted reading, and simply reading aloud to students.

The role of subskills in learning to read has stimulated considerable controversy and misconception. Since most instructional programs for beginning readers focus on subskill instruction from the outset (a practice we consider misguided), we will devote a later section to our beliefs on the role and timing of subskills in learning to read. Suffice it to say, at this point, that there is no doubt that individual learners can benefit from practice in particular skills at points in their reading development where they evidence specific problems. Thus some individuals will profit from intensive drilling (properly timed) which others will not require.

We believe that explicit teaching of activities usually termed *reading skills* should not be the initial or primary focus of a remedial reading program, especially for functionally illiterate adults, whose delicate self-concepts demand immediate and constant success and reinforcement. This viewpoint places us at variance with the emphasis in many adult literacy classes.

## Reading as a Vision-Thinking Process

Adherents to this view regard reading as an essentially visual act. They place primary emphasis on what the reader does with his eyes. There is no argument, of course, that reading *is* a visual process; the question is how important are the visual aspects of reading in comparison with its other aspects?

There is little doubt that it is helpful to know what the eye is able to accomplish during fluent reading. It is equally important to be aware of what the eye *cannot* accomplish. Smith (1975) discusses some relevant experimentation pertaining to "visual and non-visual information." The distinction between these terms is important, Smith explains, because the reader can trade one for the other. The more nonvisual information the reader can supply in terms of cognitive structure or background information, the less he needs to rely on his vision. The less background information he can bring to bear on a particular printed message, the more attention he needs to focus directly on the print. Smith explains further:

> The trade-off between visual and non-visual information in reading is critical because there is a limit to the rate at which the brain can "process" incoming

visual information, a limit often overlooked because we tend to think that we see everything that happens before our eyes. We are not usually aware that the sole function of the eye is to pick up and transmit information from the visual world to the brain. The brain has the job of making the perceptual decisions about what we see.   [p. 51]

If we can assume that a reader has reasonably normal vision, the difference between effective and ineffective reading is much more a matter of what the brain does than what the eye does, because "the brain sees when the eye is inactive."

As a focal point in his discussion of visual information processing, Smith describes a "classical experiment" in letter and word identification, originally reported by James Cattell in 1885. A subject is seated in front of a screen in an experimental laboratory. For a brief instant (between approximately a one-hundredth of a second, the minimum amount of time needed by the eye to register information, and not more than a fifth of a second, to prevent the eye from moving to a second fixation), the subject is presented with a sequence of twenty-five random letters, such as the following:

K Y B V O D U W G P J M S Q T X N O G M C T R S O

Immediately after this presentation is over, the subject is asked to report the letters in the display, as many as he can. Typically, a subject will report a four- or five-letter sequence, something like J M S Q T.

Thus it may be concluded that only four or five unrelated letters may be identified at a single fixation. It is further significant that it takes the brain a full second to process this information. When the subject is distracted by a second letter presentation (or some other interruption) before a full second has elapsed, he will usually be unable to report the full four or five letters from the initial display.

The subject is now exposed to two additional experimental displays, within the same time frame as the experiment just described. The first contains five or six unrelated words, such as:

READY        JUMP        WHEAT        POOR        BUT        SEEK

In this situation, the subject will generally recognize not four or five letters but two words, such as WHEAT and POOR, containing a total of nine or ten letters. How was he able to see twice as many letters? Since four or five letters represent as much visual information as the brain can process from one fixation, the brain must be supplying an equivalent amount of nonvisual information in order to "see ten letters' worth of words" (Smith, p. 53).

As a final experiment, the subject is exposed to, say, a twenty-five-letter display in which the letters form a meaningful sentence, such as:

KNIGHTS RODE HORSES INTO WAR

Interestingly, the subject can usually repeat the entire sentence after the same exposure for which he previously reported only four or five letters or two words. He has greatly extended the nonvisual information he brings to bear on the task.

Discussion of the nature of the nonvisual information a subject employs in the last two experiments will be postponed until the following section. For the moment, suffice it to say that the role of vision in reading may not be as great as is often suggested. It may be more accurate to say—to quote psychologist Paul Kolers (1973)—that reading is only "incidentally visual."

The purpose of this section is not to convince teachers (especially of adult remedial readers) that they should no longer be concerned about the visual behavior of their students. Certainly, if a reader has visual defects that hinder his ability to focus on the printed page, this will create a reading handicap which should be corrected. We believe, however, that much of the emphasis on improving the performance of the eyes in reading is both unnecessary and misplaced.

What instructional implications can be derived from increased insight into the role of the eyes in reading—from the knowledge that much of the credit often attributed to the eyes really belongs to the brain? It seems to us that once it is determined that the reader can see the print without undue strain, he need not be exposed to activities aimed primarily at causing adjustments in his visual approach to reading. As suggested by experiments discussed in this section, instructional approaches are often directed at what the student does with his *eyes* when the real issue is what he does with his *brain*. Furthermore, some points of emphasis, such as increasing a student's eye span, his number of fixations, or the rate of transition between fixations, etc., are virtually useless due to physiological limitations or, simply, impractical uses of instructional time. Fixation transition, for example, involves less than 10 percent of the time which elapses during reading. The bulk of time elapses *within* the separate fixations, as the brain processes information the eyes have already seen. Thus, even if it were possible to devise methods of increasing fixation transitions, such procedures would not have a significant effect on increasing reading speed or fluency.

## Reading as a Language-Thinking Process

Supporters of this psycholinguistic viewpoint stress that reading is a communication process in which the reader must process print in a manner similar in many respects to the way in which a listener processes speech. Furthermore, the ability to process print relies heavily on spoken language development. It has been widely noted that persons with advanced oral language development tend to be more effective readers than persons without this development. One recent research study with adult remedial readers suggests, in fact, that some aspects of linguistic ability correlate more highly with reading success than does ability in logical judgment.

Bosco (1977) took independent measures of "logical judgment," supposedly separated from reading comprehension, and "conservation of linguistic structure" (ability to judge the equivalence or nonequivalence of two sentences, one in the active voice, the other in the passive voice), and compared them with the same subjects' scores on reading comprehension sections of the California Achievement Test. Some excerpts from the research report highlight the results relevant for our purposes:

> The data revealed that adults do function at different levels of logical judgment and that this functioning level is independent of adults' reading achievement scores. This finding validates the feelings of many adult education teachers that their students' cognitive functioning levels are not always related to their reading scores and that their reading levels are not good predictors of their functioning level. . . .
>
> The study's third objective focused on the potential relationship between an adult's linguistic conservation ability and his reading level. The study found that these two variables were indeed significantly related. The relationship of linguistic conservation and reading achievement is especially worth noting because performances on the Linguistic Conservation instrument and on the California Achievement Test were not similar in stimulus and response characteristics. In the Linguistic Conservation task the sentence pairs were read to the students, while in the CAT the students read the materials to themselves. In addition, the types of responses varied from a closed multiple choice on the CAT to an open-ended constructed response on the Linguistic Conservation instrument. Nonetheless, the two abilities, linguistic conservation and reading, seem to parallel one another in adult populations.
>
> This finding suggests to adult reading teachers that reading problems may be related to the adult's inability to conserve linguistic structure, or more simply to his ability to ascertain semantic equivalence when the language structure is altered. The implication for instruction might be a greater emphasis upon linguistic structure, rather than upon discrete word units in the teaching of reading.  [p. 65]

As we will discuss later, correlations do not assure causality. Nonetheless, the contention that language development is a prerequisite for reading ability is supported by logic. Language ability is closely related to conceptual development. The reader with a fully developed oral language is more likely to have the conceptual ability, background experiences, and knowledge of how words interact that are essential to effective reading. He has the ability to anticipate the printed message, to make predictions as he reads, and to confirm or revise them upon reference to the text.

The importance of prediction in reading should not be underestimated, since it considerably reduces the task of the reader by allowing for the "prior elimination of unlikely alternatives." The fluent reader, in this view of the reading process, continually makes high-percentage predictions in three areas: spelling, syntax, and meaning; and, not surprisingly, is remarkably accurate in all three.

Although these processes occur simultaneously in fluent reading, they can be illustrated by three separate activities. The first, focusing on spelling predictability, is derived from a study by Miller, Brunner, and Postman (1954) and includes a series of letter groups, each comprising three "nonwords" which differ in the degree to which they approximate English spelling patterns. The second and third activities focus upon the predictability of syntax and meaning in language. They involve nonsense sentences and scrambled combinations of words.

Consider the following nonword rows and identify in each three-word group, the nonword which is most wordlike.

| | | |
|---|---|---|
| VTULPZOX | STANJUGOP | RICANING |
| VTYEHULO | VERNALIT | OZHGPMTZ |
| MOSSIANT | EINOAASE | DELGQMNW |
| IYDEWAKN | POKERSON | GFUJXZAQ |
| ONETICUL | WXPAUJVB | RPITCQUET |
| OMNTOHCH | VQWBVIFX | ATEDITOL |
| APHYSTER | DHEHHSNO | CVGJCDHM |
| RESEMPOIN | TERVALLE | MFRSIWZE |
| EJOYOEVZ | ISSAAESPW | CULATTER |
| ITYENEE | PREVERAL | GFXRWMXR |
| OAENSTVT | BHTUNQK | FAVORIAL |
| LYMISTIC | ANROAHOW | NHIDCFRA |
| HHJHUFSW | OTATIONS | YWDNMIIE |
| IJHBWSTT | INFOREMS | IODTIRPS |
| HNGTTEDE | EXPRESPE | EAPMZCEN |

This can be done with near perfect accuracy (in terms of English spelling patterns) by anyone who is familiar with English — by anyone who reads the English language. Although most of us would be incapable of making a very articulate statement if asked what we know about spelling patterns in English, the fact is that we have a tremendous amount of implicit knowledge about what letters occur in what combinations in our written language. If a word begins with $t$, for example, there are not twenty-six realistic alternatives for the second letter; the chances that it will be a vowel (five choices) or an $h$ or $r$, for example, are likely. On the other hand, the chances that it will be a $b$, $p$, or a $z$ are remote. If the word begins with $th$, a different set of odds applies to the third letter, but the chances are certainly not random.

Because of his implicit knowledge (nonvisual information) of spelling, the reader does not need to focus carefully on each individual letter. He already knows, within definite limits, what letters are likely to occur within a particular environment. He also knows implicitly that some letters occur much more frequently than others. The letter $e$, for example, occurs forty times as often as the letter $z$ (see Smith, 1971, p. 22).

The fluent reader also possesses implicit knowledge of syntax. Consider the following statement, which includes "nonwords" from the preceding exercise:

THE TERVALLE IS RICANING THE MOISSANT IN THE CULATTER BECAUSE THE MOISSANT IS LYMISTIC AND FAVORIAL.

Now answer the following questions:

1. Who is ricaning the moissant?
2. Why is the tervalle ricaning the moissant?
3. How is the moissant described in the passage?

Although neither the statement nor the question has any meaning (except that generated by the grammatical structure), the questions are not difficult to answer because of the predictability of the grammatical patterns to persons familiar with the English language.

Make a sentence using all of the following words:

CAT MOUSE ROOM ACROSS THE THE THE CHASED.

Most people write: "The cat chased the mouse across the room." But why not "The mouse chased the cat across the room" or "The room chased the cat across the mouse"? Both alternatives have exactly the same grammatical structure, but they do not fit our knowledge of the world. The point is that the reader has a sense of what word orders are reasonable from his general background experience as well as from his syntactic knowledge. (For elaboration of both of these issues, see Pearson and Johnson, 1978.)

The fluent reader continuously employs his prior knowledge of spelling patterns and word order, and his total background experience. Based on simultaneous use of these mutually supportive cue systems, he conducts himself along the lines of the scientific method. He samples the print, hypothesizes, and samples the print again in order to confirm or reject and revise his hypothesis in a continuous process. His background experience in spelling, word order, and meaning allows him to rely heavily on non-visual information. This presumably explains why a typical experimental subject is able to read a full sentence, such as "Knights rode horses into war," in the same time that he can identify four or five unrelated letters from a display. The reader uses his brain more than his eyes.

It is important to note, in this discussion of what the fluent reader does when he reads, that fluency often has as much to do with the materials to be read as with the person reading. The reader can use spelling, word order, and meaning cue systems effectively only when he is reading material which offers cues consistent with his prior experience with printed language. A normally fluent reader, for example, would often be lost in a medical journal because of his lack of familiarity with its concepts and technical terms. A person who is unfamiliar with poetry is similarily confused by its frequently unconventional syntax (compared to that of prose) and its use of ambiguous and symbolic terms. In both cases the reader's lack of familiarity with the cue systems employed in a particular printed message or, more specifically, the absence of these cue systems in the patterns to which he is accustomed, limits his ability to read effectively. Because of his lack of background knowledge, he is forced to focus on individual words at the cost of overall fluency and meaning—precisely the predicament of most beginning and remedial readers.

In their article "A Psycholinguistic View of the Fluent Reading Process," Cooper and Petrosky (1976) enumerate ten strategies of the fluent or skilled reader. Their list is an adequate summary of our conceptualization of reading as a language-thinking process, as well as a highlighting of additional points of emphasis.

1.  The reader discovers the distinctive features in letters, words, and meaning.
2.  The reader takes chances—risks errors in order to learn about printed text and to predict meaning.
3.  The reader reads to identify meaning rather than to identify words.
4.  The reader guesses from context at unfamiliar words or else just skips them.
5.  The reader takes an active role, bringing to bear his or her knowledge of the world and of the particular topic in the text.
6.  The reader reads as though he or she expects the text to make sense.
7.  The reader makes use of redundancies—orthographic, syntactic, and semantic—to reduce uncertainty about meaning.
8.  The reader maintains enough speed to overcome the limitations of the visual processing and memory systems.
9.  The reader shifts approaches for special materials.
10. The reader shifts approaches depending on the (his) purpose. (Does he want to acquire a general impression or as much specific information as possible?) [pp. 191-95]

A language-thinking view of reading dictates holistic teaching strategies that focus upon full contexts of print and upon the assumptions that, in the final analysis, reading is learned to a much greater extent than it is taught. Rather than begin with individual letter sounds and other "rules" for decoding printed symbols to spoken language, the novice reader starts by learning to read at sight a few simple phrases which appear in a natural language context and focuses on content which is meaningful to him. Often these phrases are dictated by the learner himself (language-experience approach), enabling him to begin to apply his implicit knowledge of spoken language to print. As the reader gains in confidence and in his sense of what reading is, he progresses to harder content. Although some instruction in subskills may be relevant to an individual's learning needs as he works to refine particular aspects of his reading ability, basically the student "learns to read by reading." This occurs under the watchful guidance of a tutor, who helps him identify his reading needs, answers his questions, and assists him in locating suitable materials.

Teaching strategies that are consistent with the language-thinking view of reading will be discussed in much greater detail in later chapters devoted to our instructional design.

## Conclusion

We have discussed three alternative views of the reading process in an effort to accomplish two primary objectives:

1.  To illustrate the diversity in viewpoints about how reading is accomplished by fluent readers, how it is learned, and how it can best be taught.
2.  To stress that a teacher's conceptualization of reading (even if unconscious) has a definite impact on his instructional approach.

We readily acknowledge that reading may be described in a variety of other ways. It has been described, for example, as a *perceptual process*, though usually when this term is used the focus is limited to word recognition. Reading has also been discussed as *associational learning* and as *information processing*—terms which seem to reflect the relatively sudden interest of two different schools of psychology in the reading process. While we find few bones of contention with advocates of the latter two conceptualizations, and recognize that they contribute new terminology to speculation about the reading process, we are not aware of any distinctive insights which have not been included in our discussion. Reading is also, of course, widely discussed in terms of various cultural factors likely to have an effect on the reading success of students with varying backgrounds. These discussions, however, have little to say directly about the reading process itself.

# The Role of Subskills in Learning to Read

As indicated earlier, most reading-instructional programs rely heavily on explicit teaching of various subskills, especially for beginning readers.

Since the role of explicitly taught subskills in learning to read is a topic of considerable debate among practitioners, this section is devoted to an expansion of our views on this matter.

Most persons learn to read, despite the fact that they are taught by a variety of instructional procedures and by teachers who differ widely in their assumptions about the reading process. Many professionals, confident that they know how to teach reading, point proudly to students who have learned while being taught by methods that emphasize carefully sequenced subskills. Is this evidence that all of us who have had successful students know how reading should be taught? More likely it suggests that none of us really knows how reading is learned.

This section also examines the possibility that many highly acclaimed methods for teaching reading, despite their apparently successful results, may be incidental or even at cross-purposes to learning. Further, it supports the contention introduced earlier that the crucial elements of reading are learned to a much greater extent than they are taught and that much subskill instruction is either incidental to learning to read or presented too early in this process to be maximally effective.

A review of the multitude of methods for teaching reading which are practiced in schools, all of which have "produced" successful readers, reveals very few universally common elements. It can be generally presumed that the individual who has learned to read *wanted* to learn, was liberally and continually exposed to print, and usually had access to a more experienced reader who served him as a resource person. These appear to be all the characteristics that are shared by the wide variety of reading-instructional programs. This is not to say that no other factors may help (or hinder) the efforts of beginning readers. It does suggest, however, that teachers may be too quick to accord their students' reading success to particular teaching methods which place emphasis on the mastery of specific subskills.

## Difficulties in Attributing Learning to Teaching

Although the world abounds with instructional methods for teaching beginning reading (one textbook, Aukerman [1971], describes more than fifty), and each has its share of vocal advocates, there are potential dangers in attributing successful learning primarily to the merits of any particular teaching approach. This is true in any subject matter, but particularly in regard to a language process, such as reading, where there is considerable debate as to exactly what skills the successful learner must master to accomplish his task. Too much confidence in a specific teaching method, particularly one involving an intricate hierarchy of skills to be mastered by the learner, involves at least two pitfalls.

In the first place, as Frank Smith (1973) notes, learning often occurs for reasons other than those we think:

> All too often we get results for reasons we do not suspect. . . . Similarly the fact that correlations exist between particular practices and instructional outcomes does not mean that a casual relationship exists. There is probably a high correlation between reading ability and the absence of cavities but this does not mean that tooth brushing is an essential part of learning to read.   [p. 6]

This statement suggests that a student who learns to read, after being "taught" a series of rules and performing a variety of repetitive exercises focusing upon phonics applications, may not have learned as a direct consequence of this instruction. He may, instead, have experienced enough exposure to print to have learned to read on his own; implicitly forming his own rules about how written language "works." Thus he has learned not because of his instruction but in spite of it. Although no one knows exactly how the rules of language are implicitly formulated, in either his own mind or someone else's, it is likely (as Smith also says) that the rules the student learns are quite different from those the teacher tries to teach. Thus, though we may never know exactly what rules and subskills one must master in learning to read, we know that most persons absorb them eventually, upon sufficient exposure to print.

Another fallacy in attributing learning success to teaching method is related but more complex. Teachers who think they know how to teach beginning reading are often inclined to impose their own logic upon the reading task in a manner which purports to dictate what the reader must know in order to read. This type of reasoning is illustrated in the following objection made against "assisted reading" (an approach to teaching beginning reading which involves no explicit teaching of subskills) as quoted by a Virginia state department reading specialist, in correspondence with the author.

> The assisted approach is not valid, in my opinion, because I do not see how a person can become an independent reader by constant repeating of words or sentences read to him. I feel that every person learning to read needs some word attack skills in order to read words on his own and thereby become an independent reader.

This writer is imprisoned by his position. He has declared assisted reading "not valid" because it does not appeal to his logic; he declines comment on the rationale for the approach and evidence of its success, both of which are presented in the article to which he reacted. Assisted reading is "not valid," apparently, because it differs from the method(s) with which this critic has had success in teaching. This viewpoint would seem to suggest that the beginning reader cannot learn in any manner which does not seem logical to his teacher — a dangerous assumption, considering how little is known about the learning process. Although the teacher needs to develop some working assumptions about how the novice reader approaches print, he should be wary of rejecting strategies simply because they don't appeal to his logic.

## Intermediate Learning Steps

Since no one knows exactly how reading is accomplished, it is unfair to the beginning reader to limit his opportunities to understand how written language works by insistence that he learn a particular hierarchy of skills which happen to seem logical to a person who knows how to read. The probability exists that many subskills taught in reading instruction are either unnecessary to the reading process or are taught at a time when they confuse, more than help, the learner. Every remedial reader, and especially the adult illiterate, has been troubled by the abstraction involved in deriving meaning from print. As discussed earlier, subskill instruction at the beginning stages of learning to read tends to complicate this problem. This can be crippling to the delicate self-concept of the adult functional illiterate at a time when he needs to experience success with reading, however limited, in a full and meaningful context.

In support of our belief that many "intermediate" steps in learning to read may not need to be taught directly, if in fact they are essential to learning at all, we draw several examples from the experiences of young children. Interestingly, adults don't normally feel compelled to devise intermediate steps in order to help children learn many complex concepts. A three-year-old can identify most dogs he sees, even though dogs differ significantly in any number of respects, including size, length of hair, color, etc. This is true despite the fact that no child is given an intricate list of features possessed by dogs and not by other animals. Not even an adult can explain precisely how he is able to know a dog is a dog, as opposed to a cat, and yet he is able to distinguish between them with flawless accuracy. Any definition which included all dogs and eliminated all other animals would use the language of biological classification, not that of experience. This distinction is emphasized by John Ciardi in *How Does a Poem Mean?*, using an illustration from Dickens's *Hard Times*:

> "Bitzer," said Thomas Gradgrind, "your definition of a horse."
> "Quadruped. Gramnivorous. Forty teeth, namely twenty-four grinders, four eye-teeth, and twelve incisive. Sheds coat in the spring; in marshy countries, sheds hoofs too. Hoofs hard, but requiring to be shod with iron. Age known by marks in mouth." (Thus and much more)
> "Now girl number twenty," said Mr. Gradgrind, "you know what a horse is."

The only information that children require from adults in learning to identify dogs and cats is appropriate labeling whenever they encounter either animal, and confirmation or correction from adults of their attempts to identify these animals correctly. No one knows exactly what "subskills" or "intermediate steps" are necessary to identify and distinguish animals. We do know that most people are successful when motivated, encouraged, and given feedback on their efforts to learn, without being told in any detail how they should proceed.

As the child matures, his ability to conceptualize and to form categories becomes more intricate and complex. He no longer merely identifies a dog, for example, but comes gradually to think of it differently in separate contexts. Under different circumstances, a dog may represent a pet, a friend, a responsibility, an expense, a source of fear, etc. Again, this learning is accomplished with only minimal and often incidental assistance from adults.

Certainly the effort to make sense of print is a highly complex and abstract task, in which the learner requires a good deal of feedback and reinforcement. Still, the ability of children to master other complicated undertakings with minimal assistance suggests that much reading instruction is unnecessarily complicated by undue emphasis on the mastery of subskills which are not clearly related to reading success.

Much misconception about the role of skill building in reading instruction results from faulty interpretations of correlations (for example) between knowledge of phonics or syllabication and word-recognition ability. Because good readers ("word callers") have also been shown to be more knowledgeable than poor readers about identifying sound-symbol correspondences and dividing words into syllables, these skills are often said to be prerequisites for learning to read. It is undoubtedly true that good readers are better at phonics, syllabication, and numerous other skills than poor readers—probably because it is easier to identify sounds in words if one can read them.

## Timing of Subskills

Even in instances where explicit instruction in reading subskills might be helpful to beginning readers in acquiring implicit knowledge of written language, it is frequently ineffective at the time when it is presented. The student is often asked to master parts before he has any sense of the whole to which they relate. Although such learning has been accomplished by rote memorization, with varying degrees of success, it often has a minimal impact in both meaningfulness and functional value.

Although there is ample evidence that learning processes proceed from gross approximation to gradual refinement, reading instruction is often organized, as Forrester (1977) observes, as if the reverse were true. A child who is learning to walk, to skate, or to swim begins with clumsy efforts to master the process as a whole, then focuses on refining individual parts of it. When learning to swim, for example, one cannot afford the luxury of concentrating on each arm and leg movement until one (at some level) has mastered the overall process of swimming. Only at this point can the beginning swimmer focus on individual movements in an effort to improve his overall "fluency," and only at this point do these subskills have any meaning for him.

To carry the analogy of swimming a bit farther, it is interesting to note the role of teaching in facilitating the process. It's questionable what can actually be taught to the beginning swimmer about the total activity; he may be given some helpful hints and encouragement, but he cannot be explicitly taught a series of subskills which he consciously memorizes and integrates in the beginning stages of learning to swim. He simply experiments and gradually "catches on." He masters the overall process, somewhat awkwardly at first, then sets about refining it. At this point, the teaching of subskills may be much more productive and helpful for the learner. Having approximated the overall process of learning to swim, the learner may now be taught to refine it by having his attention separately directed to various key aspects, strengthening his kick, for example, or coordinating his breathing and limb movements.

Reading subskills should be presented to the learner only as he requires them to improve his reading ability — not in a manner which tries to insist that he learn in a particular way. Learning becomes meaningful when it is clear to the learner how it relates to what he knew before and how it will help him achieve fluency. A beginning reader, for example, does not require knowledge of letter names to identify words. In fact, the nonreader has little interest in letters, until he realizes that they are necessary to the existence of words.

The teacher who imposes arbitrary and poorly timed subskills upon youthful readers may have little harmful impact on most of his students, who will eventually learn to make sense of print, regardless of the methods used to instruct them. He may, however, cause much greater difficulties for the struggling adult remedial reader, for whom skills and exercises may too quickly become an end in themselves. As noted, when an individual fails to learn to read, it seems safe to say that he has been unable to master the abstraction involved in interpreting printed symbols. Frequently teachers respond to such a situation by intensifying the abstraction — by hitting the learner where he already hurts.

There are thus substantial questions about the wisdom of a heavy diet of phonics drills and exercises for the adult illiterate who is required to work on relatively meaningless abstract tasks because he is not yet considered ready to read real words in sentences. Such procedures may not only be ineffective but may also severely demoralize the adult student.

## Learning Language without Instruction

It seems likely that the problem with many approaches to reading instruction is too much emphasis on teaching and not enough opportunity for learning without interruption and diversion. In this context, it may be helpful to examine the experience of children who have learned to read before attending school and without being taught, and also how children learn to speak. These processes offer additional insights which seem to be relevant for the instruction of adult illiterates.

Durkin (1961), Huey (1968), and Torrey (1973) document cases of preschoolers who have learned to read without being formally taught. Their conclusions suggest that early readers do not necessarily have superior intelligence but that the crucial factors influencing their success are personality, attitude, availability of reading matter, and access to persons who read to them and answer their questions. In any case, it seems that children's success in learning to read without being taught should give pause to those who advocate the necessity of instructional methods that stress the sequential mastery of specific sets of reading subskills.

This does not prove, of course, that some students are not helped by being taught certain subskills explicitly when they have a specific need for them. However, it creates substantial doubt about assumptions that the teaching of subskills is essential to the process of learning to read. This is particularly true of sound-symbol correspondences, which many instructional programs suggest are crucial in beginning reading. Such assumptions ignore the fact that deaf persons learn to read English and that many other languages (Chinese, for example) are ideographic and have no sound-symbol correspondences at all.

The experience of readers who learn without formal instruction lends weight to the argument that a person learns to read in a manner parallel to that in which a child learns to speak. Except by providing him with labels for certain objects and actions which interest him, no one really teaches a child to speak. Parents and other experienced speakers expose the child continually to verbal expressions of language, not in isolated sounds and words but in fluent sentences, spoken in full and flowing syntax. After a series of progressively successful efforts to produce sentences of his own, and helpful encouragement from experienced speakers, the child achieves an impressive facility with spoken language.

It is apparent that neither early readers nor children learning to speak receive explicit instruction in subskills. Both, however, appear to benefit significantly from access to resource persons who can answer their questions and give them feedback when they need it—after they have begun to make sense of language. At this point, beginning speakers and readers are ready to profit from specific information about separate components of language which will contribute to their overall fluency.

## Conclusion

This section has drawn heavily on the learning experiences of children to illustrate our contention that too much emphasis in classroom situations is often placed upon teaching, sometimes at the expense of learning. As noted, the functional illiterate's concept of himself as a learner is extremely delicate. He has usually been frustrated by failure in any previous school experience and approaches his present learning situation with a severe lack of self-confidence, and often with little moral support from his living and working environments. It is crucial then, especially for the adult illiterate, that he experience success as soon and as continuously as possible—that he not be forced to learn skills, with which he may have difficulty, before he sees their relevance and before he gains confidence in himself as a learner.

In summary, we believe that an effective reading-instructional program should begin with a full language context and proceed from the global to the specific. Subskill instruction should be introduced only as required by each learner, when he has acquired an overall sense of how reading works. He should be instructed in a subskill only as he evidences a need for it and only as he understands where it fits in a full reading perspective.

This teaching approach is not only consistent, we believe, with how people learn but it protects the delicate self-concept of the adult remedial reader.

The rationale for subskill instruction outlined in this chapter underlies our instructional design, especially those strategies relating to word identification described in Phase II.

# Chapter 4

# The Instructional Program

Any successful teaching-learning situation must take into account the nature of both the material to be learned and the learners themselves. Although this may seem to be an obvious statement, we believe that many educational programs for adult remedial readers are less than maximally effective because of their failures to address adequately one or both of these considerations.

## Problems with Existing Programs

Frequently, it seems, remedial reading programs focus on lists of supposed reading skills without establishing how these skills relate to the reading process. They also tend to ignore the special characteristics which make the adult remedial reader distinct from the preadult.

The first difficulty referred to above—teaching reading skills which may not be tied to any consistent view of the reading process or how people learn this process—was discussed in the preceding chapter. Heavy initial emphasis on subskills (sounds of individual letters, syllabication, etc.) may cause the beginning reader to become unnecessarily frustrated by abstractions he cannot comprehend, and diverted from the task at hand: making sense of print. This initial focus on specifics runs counter to the global to specific direction in which learning occurs—the only means by which the student can relate his new learning to his previous knowledge.

Cooper and Petrosky (1976) illustrate the failure to relate the teaching of reading skills to the reading process at another level. They excerpt the following "typical list of reading comprehension skills" from a "recent widely used textbook in developmental reading" (*Improving Reading in Every Class*, Thomas and Robinson, 1972):

1. Grasping directly stated details or facts
2. Understanding main ideas
3. Grasping the sequence of time, place, ideas, events, or steps
4. Understanding and following directions
5. Grasping implied meanings and drawing inferences
6. Understanding character (emotional reactions, motives, personal traits) and setting
7. Sensing relationships of time, place, cause and effect, events, and characters
8. Anticipating outcomes
9. Recognizing the author's tone, mood, and intent
10. Understanding and drawing comparisons and contrasts
11. Drawing conclusions or making generalizations
12. Making evaluations   [p. 196]

Cooper and Petrosky then comment:

The striking thing about this list is that it has nothing to say about the reading process, even though it appears in a book entitled *Improving Reading in Every Class*. The list does not mention language and it has nothing to say about processing information—identifying meaning—from print during the act of reading. The list does not help us think about what a reader does during reading and, therefore, it is likely to mislead us about what we can do to help readers. [p. 196]

In addition to the problems that face learners when they confront tasks which are inconsistent with the reading process or fragment that process unnecessarily, adult functional illiterates are often handicapped by instructors who teach them as if they were children. This is not surprising in view of the fact that many adult remedial readers are enrolled in part-time programs guided by teachers who work primarily with children in their regular jobs. Nonetheless, this inflexibility in teaching approach may not only demoralize the adult student but fail to build upon his assets and to address his needs.

Having cited some frequent difficulties encountered in instructional programs for adult remedial readers, we will summarize our observations and assumptions relating to the reading and learning-to-read processes and to the adult as a remedial reader. They are the basis for our overall instructional design.

# Reading Process Implications
# for Instructional Design

As indicated in the previous chapter, we believe that reading is a language-thinking process which draws heavily on the individual's linguistic abilities. It is thus especially important that the beginning reader be exposed to a full context of written language so that he may understand the nature and purpose of the reading act and the similarities between print and speech. Since no one knows exactly how the individual learns to read or to speak, it is important that the adult remedial reader not be burdened initially with any teaching approach which demands that he learn in a particular manner or according to any prescribed sequence of steps.

Natural written language must not be fragmented to the extent that the beginning reader no longer has the opportunity to formulate and test his own hypotheses about how reading works. As discussed in the previous chapter, while we don't know exactly what rules the mind formulates to cope with written language, we observe that most people eventually learn to read (though taught by a variety of instructional methods or, in some cases, not taught at all) when motivated and exposed to print on a continuous basis. We must thus assure that the teaching approaches we employ for beginning readers do not deny them the possibility of gaining insights into reading in ways we may not anticipate.

As the novice reader begins to make sense of print through the holistic strategies discussed in this chapter under Phase I, he may be in a position to profit from selected subskill instruction within the frameworks we describe under Phase II. In this manner, decoding is mastered in the same global-to-specific direction as other learning occurs. In Phase II, the beginning reader is in a position to benefit from explicit subskill instruction (though the amount and type differs for each individual), because he understands where particular skills fit into his overall efforts to achieve fluency and can relate them to what he already knows. Since he is able to use context more effectively, and because he now expects reading to make sense, the learner can more effectively predict meaning from print and also identify difficult sounds and words through "prior elimination of unlikely alternatives."

In Phase III the student's primary intent is not increasing his decoding skills but acquiring information. At this point the emphasis is upon reading to learn, rather than learning to read. Again, the direction of learning is global to specific. When reading for information, one must first achieve some conceptual framework for the subject matter. Only in this manner is the reader able to formulate "advance organizers" which allow him to place new information in perspective.

# Reader Characteristics as Implications for Instructional Design

As suggested in previous chapters, the adult functional illiterate has a number of distinctive characteristics which need to be considered in any instructional program designed to meet his needs. While it is true that not all of the characteristics listed here are unique to the adult as a remedial reader, and many are overlapping, all are factors which are important in the adult's case and need to be taken into account. These factors may be divided under three headings: learning assets, practical needs, and learning liabilities. While all the factors grouped under these headings have been referred to in previous chapters, it seems appropriate to summarize the information in each category which seems especially relevant to the planning of instructional programs.

## Learning Assets

Many instructional designs seem to be conceptualized in a manner which suggests that their only purpose is to eliminate the deficits of the learner; the assets of the learner are frequently overlooked or discounted. The assets of the adult remedial reader are often considerable and should not be ignored in any effort to help him.

By virtue of his extended years of living, the adult functional illiterate inevitably approaches reading with a broader background of experience than the beginning child reader. While this fact may not be of significant immediate value for the adult who has never been exposed to print before, breadth of background experience will certainly be of benefit to the adult student in comprehending print as his decoding ability progresses. Lack of background experience, in fact, is one of the primary deficits noted in children who evidence comprehension difficulties (Harris and Smith, 1976, p. 52).

As a reflection of his wide range and depth of background experiences, the adult remedial reader frequently possesses a vocabulary which far surpasses his measured levels in other reading-related abilities. The fact that the functional illiterate has a large store of spoken words, and the concepts that these words represent, is a distinct advantage to him as he learns to read, especially when he focuses on printed matter which pertains to his areas of interest and expertise.

Perhaps the greatest asset of the adult remedial reader is the fact that he is motivated to accomplish specific reading objectives. He is not in class to learn to read because someone else thinks this is what he ought to do. He is there to learn to overcome obstacles which handicap him in his personal life or his work. The fact that the adult learner is involved in reading instruction because he chooses to be, and is engaged in the pursuit of personally meaningful goals, is an asset which can be built upon in any teaching-learning situation.

## Practical Needs

The adult functional illiterate approaches instruction with certain practical needs which should be taken into account in any program designed to teach him. In addition to the fact that he requires instruction tailored closely to his personal living (or occupational) objectives, he needs immediate payoff. He needs to leave each session with a sense of satisfaction and the knowledge that he has learned something specific, so that he can see real progress in the direction of his goals. This ideal, of course, cannot always be achieved, but it should be kept in mind during teacher planning. In the meantime, it is wise, at the beginning of the adult's involvement with reading instruction, to explain carefully to him that progress at first is likely to be extremely slow, sometimes hardly noticeable, but usually accelerates dramatically after the initial period. Thus the student must be encouraged to temper his early expectations. This will be discussed further in the section on orientation to reading instruction.

It must be remembered that the adult learner is, for the most part, extremely time conscious. His class involvement usually makes considerable inroads on what otherwise would be leisure time spent with his family and friends (a policy he must justify to them). On the other hand, if he is fortunate enough to participate in a work-release program, he has to be able to justify his instructional time to his employer and to other employees, who may be inconvenienced as a result of his participation.

Because of the pressure under which he engages in formal learning activities, the functional illiterate often imposes strict time limitations upon himself, whereby he allows only a certain period to learn to read or to make what he considers satisfactory progress. Although these time limits are frequently unrealistic for the learner's expectations, the teacher should be aware of the severe time pressure his students are apt to feel. As a result, he should design activities that assure immediate and continuous success, while, at the same time, trying to tone down unrealistic aspirations.

In the final analysis, the most compelling need of the adult functional illiterate is to achieve independence with whatever printed materials he confronts regularly in his daily life and work. Instructional planning must take into account the fact that (1) the adult student's primary motivation is not to learn reading in the abstract but to learn to derive meaning from particular printed messages, and (2) meaning is more important than precision in "word sounding" or any other similar skill.

Instruction should be arranged to allow the learner ample periods of time to work individually on real-life reading materials, receiving help from an experienced reader only as he chooses. Success is measured in terms of the student's ability to derive meaning from printed messages of interest to him, whether or not he can identify every word in these messages and regardless of how he performs on any skill test.

## Learning Liabilities

/ Like preadult remedial readers, the adult functional illiterate suffers from a number of potential learning handicaps. Primary among these is his low self-concept as a learner. Often, having never had a rewarding school experience in his life, the illiterate is apt to have little confidence in his prospect for success and tends to be easily frustrated by failure to see substantial progress, especially at the beginning of instruction. He becomes discouraged, often to the point of discontinuing his efforts, if he fails to meet goals which may be beyond his reach.

/ Another difficulty of the adult illiterate student is communication problems in his relationship with his instructor. In addition to his feelings of insecurity in the educational setting, the adult illiterate usually lives and works in environments much less verbal than those to which the teacher is accustomed. Although his vocabulary is often much stronger than that of the child nonreader, it is not up to the level of most adults, and he is not used to being bombarded with verbiage in the manner typical of many classroom environments. Lack of familiarity with the teacher's language (syntax and vocabulary), as well as the sheer volume of words, may confuse him in situations where he already feels vulnerable.

Although these learning liabilities are not easily eliminated, or even counteracted, with total success, the perceptive teacher can blunt their effects through maintenance of a nonthreatening atmosphere in which the prospect of failure is minimized. Each student must be asssured tangible success on a continuous basis. At the same time, he must receive regular feedback and constructive reinforcement for his efforts. In this manner, fears and unrealistic expectations can be tempered, so that each learner's needs may be addressed by appropriate individualized instruction.

The preceding discussions of the reading process and adult remedial reader characteristics provide the rationale upon which our instructional design is based. Our organization of teaching strategies, we believe, is consistent with what is known about the reading process and the way reading is learned. Further, it has been designed to build on the assets and needs of the functional illiterate while minimizing the effects of his learning disadvantages.

# The Continuum: Learning to Read, Reading to Learn

All persons who undertake to read fall somewhere on a continuum whose end points are learning to read and reading to learn (see figure 3). The nature and purpose of reading instruction, of course, vary, depending upon different levels of reader independence. We will list the strategies we feel are dictated by different degrees of learner independence and briefly discuss how they relate to our conceptualizations of the reading process and to the special characteristics of the adult remedial reader. Strategies are grouped into three phases, representing the left and middle (learning to read) and the right (reading to learn) segments of the continuum.

Different teaching strategies, of course, overlap to a considerable extent. In general, however, we believe that the following are the appropriate strategies to use with adult remedial readers, as they progress from left to right on the continuum of reading independence. It is certainly true that many learners may enter instruction at a reading-instructional level which can be most effectively addressed by strategies in Phase II or Phase III on the continuum. Nonetheless, even a student who has shown substantial independence may profit from a return to "lower level" strategies, to reinforce what he has previously learned or because he is focusing on more difficult reading matter.

It should be stressed that the strategies on this continuum address the teaching of reading from two basic standpoints. In Phases I and II the emphasis is on decoding, and in Phase III on comprehension. The term *emphasis* is crucial, because these two conceptualizations of reading are never completely separated. Furthermore, decoding and comprehension have a circular relationship in which comprehension not only results from decoding but precedes and supports it. Still, our strategies in Phases I and II are geared primarily toward word identification, in and out of context, and our strategies in Phase III toward reading for information and recreation. As noted earlier in this chapter, the strategies associated with each emphasis are predicated on the assumption that learning occurs in a general-to-specific direction.

Individual strategies will be discussed only briefly in this chapter, in order to describe the rationale for their assignment to instructional phases. Detailed explanations for each strategy will follow, as we elaborate on different components of the instructional design.

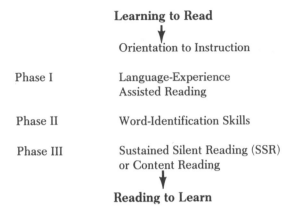

**Learning to Read**

Orientation to Instruction

Phase I              Language-Experience
                     Assisted Reading

Phase II             Word-Identification Skills

Phase III            Sustained Silent Reading (SSR)
                     or Content Reading

**Reading to Learn**

Figure 3. The Learning-to-Read Continuum

## Phase I: Language Experience and Assisted Reading

We believe that language experience and assisted reading are the strategies with which to begin teaching adults who are judged to be total nonreaders. The strategies we include under Phase I are consistent with our viewpoint that reading is a language process best learned in a global-to-specific fashion which minimizes abstraction, especially in the early stages of reader development. Reading at this learning stage may be defined as "sight recognition of words in meaningful contexts."

These beginning strategies, used individually or in combination, are also consistent with our observations relating to the adult remedial reader. The language-experience approach, in which the student dictates his own material, builds directly upon the background and speaking vocabulary of the learner, and gives him the opportunity to focus on passages that include topics, names, and terms of personal interest and concern. In assisted reading, the learner repeats words in meaningful phrases as they are pointed to and vocalized by an experienced reader. This strategy may be used effectively in conjunction with language experience and the use of materials which the learner selects for himself. It assures immediate payoff and protects the student's self-concept by virtually eliminating the possibility of failure in the beginning stages of instruction.

By virtue of its initial emphasis on language-experience and assisted reading, our instructional design attempts to establish an atmosphere conducive to early success and encouragement for the learner. The emotional climate fostered by such an atmosphere enables the adult illiterate to contend with his early insecurities while building momentum for greater challenges as his reading ability progresses.

## Phase II: Word-Identification Skills

Word-identification skills often constitute virtually total instructional programs. Beginning readers in particular are often taught these skills, to the exclusion of all other material. As we have indicated, we disagree with this approach.

There is no doubt that word-identification techniques can help many students refine their reading abilities. We believe, however, that this instruction is maximally effective only after the learner has acquired insight into the reading process, through experience with the full context of printed language pertaining to content with which he is interested and familiar. In this manner, the novice reader will not fragment the language (and increase abstraction) until he has some grasp of where the pieces fit in the puzzle. This assures that learning to decode will continue to proceed from the global to the specific. Once the novice reader has acquired a basic understanding of what reading is and how print "works," he is ready to refine his word-attack skills outside of context. Reading in Phase II is thus characterized as "refinement of word recognition ability through application of systematic decoding techniques."

The instructional program is focused upon such activities as the systematic use of contextual clues, identification of sight words out of context, phonics, and structural analysis only to the extent that the learner evidences the need for this training. As research (Hoskisson [1974], for example) and experience have suggested, beginning readers often master reading subskills on their own, simply from repeated exposure to print, without having been taught. There is no need to teach what the learner has acquired on his own.

Instruction in word identification offers appropriate means for remedial readers to receive intensive practice in areas where their experience indicates to them that they need it. When carefully planned and individualized, this training is personally relevant and offers immediate payoff toward the learner's reading independence.

## Phase III: Content Reading and Sustained Silent Reading

Content area and sustained silent reading (SSR) make up the "reading to learn" end of our instructional continuum. The term *activities* (rather than *methods*) is perhaps the most appropriate description of these teaching approaches, both of which are characterized by a high degree of learner independence.

The term *content reading* pertains to independent reading in specific subject matter areas of the student's own choosing. *Sustained silent reading*, as the term implies, involves gradually increasing the time during which an individual can read (and comprehend) silently.

When engaging in the activities of Phase III, the adult remedial reader gains knowledge and experience in real-life literacy. He is now able, to a large extent, to plan and direct his own program for continued self-improvement and increased reading independence. Reading in Phase III is thus defined as "deriving meaning from print." The reader relies heavily on his speaking vocabulary and background experience. He is able to pursue with greater independence the objectives which led him to reading instruction in the first place. He can focus directly upon newspapers, job orders, or other reading matter of his own choosing as he seeks answers to his own questions. Although the learner still requires guidance and assistance from his instructor, he is given help only when he asks for it. The focus is on independence. Reading to learn is a means to an end, not an end in itself.

In Phase III, the learner determines his own goals and measures his own progress. He is in a better position than in Phases I and II to evaluate the payoff from his efforts and (one hopes) has overcome some of his earlier insecurities. Now that the student has experienced success in word recognition and reading for meaning, learning in Phase III provides its own feedback and offers its own rewards.

## Orientation to Instruction

The field of reading abounds with literature relating to the concept of reading readiness as it pertains to children. For the most part, however, this material is not helpful or irrelevant to reading programs for adults. This is true for at least three reasons. First, the developmental stages of children, upon which many reading-readiness programs are based, are quite different from those of adults. Second, reading-readiness programs frequently involve mastery of set sequences of skills which we believe are unnecessary prerequisites for instruction. Third, a primary objective of reading readiness is often to motivate children to read. In the case of adult illiterates who have voluntarily sought or submitted to instruction, this is seldom necessary.

Established viewpoints of reading readiness are primarily concerned with the child's readiness to read in terms of his physical, psychological, and linguistic developments. The general premise is that when the child reaches prescribed maturity levels in these areas, he is most ready to learn — and to be taught — to read. These "ideal" maturity levels for reading readiness, even to the extent that they can be identified, are clearly much different for illiterate adults than for young children.

A further limitation of many existing reading-readiness programs is that they prescribe specific skills which the learner must master before he is ready to learn to read. As discussed in an earlier chapter, we are doubtful that anyone can identify a discrete list of skills which are essential to the reading process, much less a particular order in which they must be mastered. Furthermore, as we suggest in our instructional design, it may be not only irrelevant but frustrating to the novice reader, especially the time-conscious and insecure adult illiterate, to be encumbered with a series of subskills which he may not only find difficult to learn but also for which he sees no immediate purpose.

An additional aspect of many reading-readiness programs has to do with the motivational aspects of preparing children to learn to read. Such programs frequently list activities and experiences designed to increase the child's interest and appetite for learning to read. For the adult, however, motivation cannot, and need not, be stimulated in the same manner. If the adult illiterate is not motivated to learn to read, he is not likely to submit to instruction in the first place, much less participate in activities for enthusiasm building. For the adult illiterate who submits to instruction, motivation is already present; furthermore, this motivation is directed toward particular content objectives. Whereas the adult illiterate may be interested in learning to read in general (in learning to "read reading," as children are initially taught to do), his primary objective is to learn to read particular content. Thus the adult student has little need to be convinced of the importance of learning to read. He may, of course, need to be convinced that he has a reasonable prospect of success — an issue on which we will focus later.

In the remainder of this chapter we discuss a number of general considerations which must be taken into account in analyzing and increasing the preparedness of the adult illiterate for learning to read. In contrast to many detailed reading-readiness programs which have been designed for children, we make no pretense of addressing and analyzing all factors which affect the adult remedial reader's readiness for instruction. Indeed, given the diversity of adult backgrounds, motivations, developmental stages, and total life situations, this would be extremely difficult. We will attempt, instead, to draw attention to what we have observed to be some of the crucial factors in preparing adult illiterates for reading instruction and/or assuring that they are in a position to benefit from this instruction. The following discussion is divided into three subsections, focusing upon the nature of the instructional program, tempering the expectations of the learner, and the nature of print.

## The Nature of the Instructional Program

As a first order of business, the teacher should explain to the learners the nature of the program in which they will be involved together. He should describe how sessions, materials, and records are organized and the extent to which the learner's input is to be required in planning the instructional objectives and evaluating his success in meeting them. To begin to develop a sense of security about the remedial reading program, the adult illiterate must acquire a sense of perspective about how the program operates and what is expected of him as a participant.

We believe that the most effective adult remedial reading programs are those which draw to the maximum extent upon the resources of the learners and in which the learners are actively involved in planning their own, individualized learning experiences. The essence of this individualized approach is repeated conferences between the teacher and each adult participant. Such conferences serve a variety of purposes which benefit the beginning reader. On a one-to-one basis, these include assessment of the learner's particular interests and needs, selection of appropriate reading material and instructional methods, and guided teaching of skills and concepts the individual requires to accomplish his reading goals. This cycle is repeated on a continuous basis as progress is evaluated, new needs are diagnosed, and new goals are determined. Records are maintained which provide ready reference for determining what the learner has accomplished in pursuit of his objectives.

To the greatest extent possible, the learner needs to understand that he is involved in a collaborative venture. The teacher provides knowledge, guidance, and emotional support, but the learner has the primary responsibility for establishing his reading purposes and goals. It must be stressed, of course, that this arrangement is an ideal which is difficult to achieve with the typically apprehensive and insecure adult beginning reader. Often the illiterate student depends upon his teacher to establish his reading purposes and goals, and thus tends to adopt a passive role toward instruction. This situation presents the perceptive teacher with a formidable challenge. He must not intimidate the student with too many demands for independence at a time when the student does not feel ready to assert himself. At the same time, he must encourage the student to become more self-directing.

Under the individualized approach, the teacher discusses with the adult student what material he wants to read and the likelihood of his being able to deal with this material effectively, based upon test scores, informal assessments, and the student's own estimate of his reading ability. If necessary, the teacher may suggest some appropriate compromise in the learner's initial aspirations, so that the student can experience more immediate success while focusing on content which is personally meaningful to him.

## Tempering Expectations of the Learner

In previous chapters we have discussed various aspects of the frame of mind with which the adult illiterate approaches reading instruction, including the fact that he is apt to have a low concept of himself as a learner and to be prone to frustration and discouragement. In addition, he may have imposed upon himself an unrealistic timetable for success. Somewhat like the first-grader who is disappointed at not learning to read the first day of school, the adult illiterate is likely to say to himself: "I'll give it a week or two and see if I'm learning anything." Frequently, after an unrealistically short interval, he concludes that he is "not learning anything" and, embarrassed and feeling that he is wasting his time, he discontinues reading instruction.

Many times a student leaves before he has had a real chance to achieve progress. Furthermore, he may have learned (or may already know) more about reading than he realizes, but be discouraged because he cannot achieve a particular goal he has set for himself, such as identifying all the words in a newspaper article.

The remainder of this section focuses upon three separate but related issues pertaining to learner expectations: forming the initial contract, modifying aspirations, and redefining reading success.

**Forming the Initial Contract.** In our work with adult illiterates we have found it helpful to ask students to commit themselves to a specified period of instruction before they begin. We want them to understand from the outset (especially in cases of total nonreaders) that they may not see significant results for a *substantial* period and that we prefer *not* to work with them unless they agree to a specified number of hours of instruction before they judge their success. After this designated period has elapsed, we assist every individual in making a realistic assessment of progress and we accept his decision about continuing in our program.

Learning to read is a process which, especially for the non-reading adult, is extremely complicated and abstract in the early stages, but is apt to become much less so once the learner begins to achieve a minimum level of proficiency. It is therefore important that the learner be patient, that he not be hasty in judging himself a failure or letting his discouragement prevent the possibility of sudden success at a later point of instruction. As we stress to our students, we prefer to invest our time in learners who are prepared to contend with and outlast their early frustrations.

The appropriate duration of an "initial contract" is often difficult to determine. It must be long enough to permit meaningful appraisal of success and yet not so long as to become automatically self-defeating. Our experience suggests that six weeks is an appropriate period in part-time programs, where students are involved in approximately five hours of instructional time per week. The overall length of the initial contract may vary considerably, according to the teaching-learning situation, but the important thing is that teacher and student share defined expectations about the duration of their early relationship.

It must be stressed, of course, that an initial contract provides no guarantee that its terms will be adhered to. Students may drop out no matter what understanding has been reached, because of discouragement or environmental factors beyond their control. Commitment to this sort of agreement before instruction, however, increases the chance that students will persist long enough to see encouraging results. At this point, if the initial contract has been successful, the teacher may encourage adult illiterates to agree to another contract for a longer commitment.

**Modifying Aspirations.** In addition to securing a commitment from students that they plan to continue instruction for a reasonable period, the teacher is often faced with the need to modify student aspirations. The adult remedial reader who seeks instruction with unrealistic goals will often be unable to live up to his expectations within the time frame he has allowed himself and may become severely demoralized. Thus an important part of reading readiness for the adult illiterate is to acquire and maintain compatibility between his reading objectives and his reading abilities.

A real challenge for the teacher develops when the adult remedial reader's primary incentive is the prospect of mastering material beyond his existing level of competence. The teacher must then set about helping the student achieve some satisfaction in the direction of his goal while employing methods and supplementary materials which are conducive to his reading development. To ignore the student's prevailing interest would depress his morale in a learning experience already fraught with frustration and perhaps discourage him from persisting in the reading program. On the other hand, failure to use supplementary materials geared to the student's abilities and needs will hinder reading progress.

It is obviously true that if an illiterate adult's primary objective is to learn to read the Bible, a not infrequent objective among Adult Basic Education students, the teacher cannot help him become a proficient Bible reader very quickly. He can, however, give such a learner a sense that his personal concerns are being addressed by encouraging use of the Bible as a curriculum tool. This is accomplished by reading and talking with the student about the content and sound-symbol correspondences in Bible passages which interest him and by equipping him to read some Bible phrases, however simple. The student's morale may be heightened and his interest in the Bible may serve as a foundation for additional reading-improvement efforts — relevant language-experience creations, assisted reading of selected passages, or even prepackaged or programmed materials to reinforce particular reading skills. Although most of the Bible may be far beyond the student's capabilities and it may be inappropriate as a single tool for instruction, it gives some adult remedial readers a purpose for their learning and a foundation for improving their reading abilities.

**Redefining Reading Success.** An important aspect of reading readiness, especially for practical-minded and time-conscious adult illiterates, frequently has to do with their conceptions of reading itself. Often our ideas about reading stem almost entirely from our early efforts to decode print to sound. As a result, we tend to think of reading as a process of decoding with precise accuracy. The adult illiterate, whether he has attended school or not, often has a similar viewpoint. As a consequence, he is apt to feel, for example, that he cannot read a passage in which he cannot identify each word. Such a learner needs a new criterion for success.

An incident in the author's experience may illustrate this problem. I had worked with a dedicated remedial reader in a part-time program for about six months, and this student's reading independence had grown to the point where I thought he could read and understand a newspaper article of his own choosing. The student was hesitant but, after some prodding on my part, agreed to select an article and do what he could. I left him alone for perhaps fifteen minutes, then returned and asked him how he was doing.

"Terrible," he said.

"What's the trouble?" I asked, surprised.

"I just can't get it. The words are too hard."

With some misgiving that I had challenged him too severely, I glanced at the article he had selected, which dealt with plans for construction of a new hospital. I then asked a number of questions about content: Where was the hospital to be built? What size would it be? How much would it cost? Where would the money come from? The student answered each question flawlessly, without hesitation, so that it quickly became evident that his retention equaled that of a mature reader; yet he was convinced that he had been unable to read it. In the final analysis, he was disturbed about his inability to decode a few difficult words, including semitechnical terms and the names of persons. He had no difficulty comprehending the basic content.

In the adult's case, especially, the criterion for reading success is the extent to which it serves the reader's purposes. If the individual can comprehend what he wants and needs to know from a printed message, he is able to read it. He need not necessarily be able to identify every word; he needs to get meaning from the message as a whole. Well-meaning teachers often try to "teach" adults too much, without allowing them time to experiment free from teacher intervention. Every reading program should allow enough time for students to read uninterruptedly. Only in this manner can they progress in their understanding of what reading *is* and in their abilities to make sense of print.

## The Nature of Printed Language

Although the points discussed in this section apply primarily to total nonreaders, we have discovered from our experience that they cannot be taken for granted in instructing these students. Many adult illiterates are unaware of the nature of printed language and thus are unaware that a particular "clump of letters" corresponds to a particular spoken word, that print is read from left to right and top to bottom, and that a specific sequence of letters represents the same word, even though it appears in different places on a page. Although these concepts are easy to learn, they must not be ignored, or valuable instruction time may be wasted at the price of growing frustration for the learner.

To the experienced reader, the fact that a clump of letters corresponds to a spoken word is a simple idea to grasp. Similarly, an experienced reader can count the number of words he hears in a spoken sentence, because he is familiar with the written language. But as Smith (1971) observes, phonetic transcriptions of normal spoken syntax do not reveal orderly pauses between words; many words are run together, and relatively long pauses often occur between syllables in a word. The individual who can count the words spoken by another person is able to do so largely because he is familiar with their appearance in print. As Smith notes, this is virtually impossible for a lengthy utterance in a foreign language, with whose written form one is unfamiliar.

The preceding discussion has important implications for the nonreader. Although he can communicate adequately in speech, the total illiterate cannot always distinguish individual words. He may not be aware, for example, that *the* is a separate word, since he does not hear it in isolation. This situation is apt to create problems for the adult learner who is struggling to learn to read and who is asked to identify particular words or to follow and/or repeat a line of print read by someone else.

Two other potential difficulties of the total nonreader are the left-to-right and top-to-bottom orientation for print and the fact that the identity of a word does not depend on its location. The remedy for these problems is, of course, to give the reader what he lacks: exposure to full printed syntax.

In this manner it is often possible for the perceptive teacher to minimize the novice reader's early confusion, enabling him to learn more rapidly and effectively in the early stages of instruction. This may be done by reading aloud to the student, while pointing at the words and calling attention to the points discussed above, or by reading aloud as the student points to the words. A fringe benefit of these procedures is that they help the reader become accustomed to the vocabulary and syntax of written language and the manner in which they may differ from the vocabulary and syntax of his accustomed spoken language.

Although the issues discussed in this section may be relevant only to the most handicapped of beginning readers—to those comparatively few who have had virtually no experience with print—they are of crucial importance to such persons. Before charging headlong into reading instruction, the teacher must be assured that the learner has a basic understanding of the nature of print. When this has been achieved, the student is ready for the language-experience and assisted reading strategies which make up Phase I.

# Chapter 5

# Using Language for Reading (Phase I)

The language-based approach to reading instruction is tied directly to the beginning reader's oral language. The student's spoken words are converted to print and become the material for reading instruction. In this manner it is assured that the student is familiar with the vocabulary, sentence structure, and concepts he encounters in print.

## Rationale for Language Experience

Rather than dividing the reading process into a sequence of separate skills to be mastered, the premise of the language-experience approach is that reading is a component of the network of language processes — reading, speaking, writing, listening, and thinking. Proponents of the language-experience approach believe the learner's ability to deal with language in reading is directly related to his capacities to speak and to write. The emphasis is upon fluency and meaning in full language contexts. Such contexts are ordinarily provided by passages that the learner, individually or with other learners, creates through dictating his own experiences. Continued exposure to such high-interest material allows the reader to begin to break the written code.

In addition to helping the remedial reader to learn and reinforce words that are personally important to him and to improving his fluency with the written language by relating it closely to his speech, the language-experience approach may serve a more subtle purpose as well. When the adult functional illiterate becomes aware that his own life's experience has become the curriculum for his learning, this provides a substantial boost to his morale. He is stimulated to think, to produce, and to comprehend. This combination of processes serves to increase the learner's confidence and his motivation, which are powerful attributes for the beginning reader.

After the reader acquires a sense of what reading is and has experienced success with a full context of print which is meaningful to him, he is ready to refine his knowledge of word-attack skills. At this point in his individualized program of instruction (Phase II), the language-experience material which he has dictated earlier may be used as a starting point for the study of sound-symbol correspondences.

## Application for Adults

Although the language-experience approach for teaching children usually focuses on stories and inventions of the imagination, this emphasis can be modified for illiterate adults. Some adult learners readily produce straightforward material dealing with facts and incidents, relating to their own lives, which can be transcribed by the teacher. The following examples illustrate such creations:

> My name is Marvin.
> I work in Dietrick Dining Hall.
> I serve the students.
> I live in Blacksburg, Virginia.

> Me and my sister never did go to school.
> I never learned no reading before.
> But I'm getting it right good now.

These passages are significant for different reasons. The brief biographical sketch, presented first, focuses upon words that are crucial to its author's personal sight vocabulary—his name, his occupation, where he works, and where he lives. The second passage represents a radical departure from conventional syntax; nonetheless, it has been preserved in written form exactly as dictated by the speaker. This facilitates the learner's efforts to comprehend ideas in print that he can talk about.

It is frequently the case, of course, that adult illiterates who are new to the classroom situation are reluctant to express themselves freely in this manner. Under these circumstances, the teacher must casually involve them in informal discussions in order to relieve their inhibitions. This may be approached in various ways, for example, by reading aloud a story or other printed selection calculated to arouse interest or debate and by asking for student reactions.

Sometimes learners are motivated to express themselves in response to the teacher's carefully selected questions pertaining to subjects which are of interest to them. A favorite topic among older adults, for example, involves variations on the theme "how things used to be."

Another encouragement for students to generate language-experience reading material is provided by open-ended stimulus statements, such as "Last week when it snowed. . . ." This technique may be used by asking a group of persons to provide their own completions to the statement or by giving several closely related open-ended statements to one individual.

When learners are actively involved in generating potential language-experience-related material, the teacher, with the student's permission, should record student statements on a blackboard or a tape recorder for typing and duplication at the earliest opportunity.

The language-experience approach is most successful when learners can be motivated to dictate selections that are closely related to their personal experiences. Although there are no restrictions on the range of topics that are appropriate for language-experience activities, topics which might provide good stimuli are suggested by the results of a study by the Maine State Department of Education. This research indicated fourteen general areas which are apt to be of interest to Adult Basic Education students:

1. Living within my means
2. What do I do when I retire? (older students)
3. Smart food buying
4. Looking for a job
5. How can I become a better person?
6. Understanding insurance
7. Family health
8. My responsibilities as a citizen
9. Population, pollution, and conservation
10. The joy of good food
11. Growing old
12. How to build character in children
13. Spelling better
14. Using better English    [O'Donnell (1975), p. 27]

The fact that this list represents the interests of a particular group of adult remedial students does not mean that these items should necessarily become the focal points for a language-experience-based curriculum. The individual student's interests and needs should always be the focal point for his learning, and the teacher must stimulate expression of them in any way he can.

Once student products appear on paper, teacher and learners may "read" them together, the student repeating the words (his own) after the teacher, until he has made the transition from speech to print. This procedure is similar to the assisted reading technique discussed in the following section, except that the latter approach goes beyond student-generated products and focuses upon more challenging reading matter that the student encounters in his daily living and working environments.

One frequently hears the reservation, in regard to the language-experience approach to reading instruction, that learners are not reading but simply memorizing. Such sentiments seem to imply that language experience is invalid for this reason. On the contrary, memorization of text is an asset, not a hindrance, to a student's early efforts to learn to read. The objective is for the student to "see how reading works" by relating words in print to those that are already in his head. As long as he focuses on printed words in syntax that corresponds to the meaningful phrases he has memorized, this can only help him make sense of print. Not only does he learn more easily to identify certain words by sight, he becomes more accustomed to the left-to-right orientation of print and the fact that the purpose of reading is to derive meaning from, as opposed simply to sounding out, printed symbols.

## Modifications of the Language Experience

The basic language-experience approach of "dictate and read" lends itself to several modifications which may be helpful to students once they are familiar with the basic procedure. Primary among these is the "scrambled dictation" approach. In this procedure phrases dictated by the student have been given to him to read after they've been rearranged, thus assuring that he hasn't memorized them. We illustrate this point by drawing directly upon our experience with an adult illiterate with whom we worked in a work-release setting for university employees.

Herman (name changed), a thirty-eight-year-old total nonreader, was unable to recognize his name (or anything else) in print when he enrolled in our program. Over a few months, after a very slow start, he acquired the ability to read two to three dozen short language-experience passages which he had dictated at different times. (It should be added that Herman's instruction during this period was not confined to passages he dictated himself but also involved some biblical verses and other material of interest to him.) One of the shorter selections was:

> I work at Dietrick Dining Hall.
> I work every day except Friday and Saturday.
> I drive my car to work at the dining hall.

From this passage we formulated a new passage which kept the same phrase structure but prohibited the possibility of pure memorization:

> I drive my car to Dietrick Dining Hall every day except Friday and Saturday.

Although the preceding involves phrase manipulation only within the same passage, this procedure may be made more challenging (and was for Herman) by combining phrases from two or more separate passages dictated by the student at different times. Also, the instructor may on occasion interject a word or two which he suspects might be of high utility for a particular student, even though that word has not appeared in any of the student's dictation. A simple illustration, which we employed in Herman's case, is use of the student's name to replace a personal pronoun. We frequently changed Herman's statements to the third person (Herman Jenkins works at Dietrick Dining Hall . . .) in order to give him greater exposure to his own name in print.

As an alternative to inserting unfamiliar words in student-generated passages, the teacher can devise means of encouraging a student to volunteer these words. One means of doing this is to present the learner with a series of one- or two-word completion activities, such as:

MY NAME IS _____.
I LIVE IN THE CITY OF _____.
I WORK AT _____.

These statements are read to the student, who follows the line of print and supplies the appropriate word for the teacher to write in the blank space. This fill-in-the-blank procedure forces the student to focus on the printed form of a word he has been encouraged to produce himself and, therefore, may be more apt to remember.

Another extension to language experience, which involves a close tutorial relationship, is the information reading technique. This instructional method allows the learner to acquire new information while building a "reading-learning experience" (Schneiderman, 1977). After the teacher and the learner discuss what information is needed and relevant, reading material is selected. The instructor then reads the material to the learner in small segments, perhaps a paragraph at a time. After teacher and learner have discussed and clarified the content of the material, the student states what he has learned or has understood which he considers important. Student statements are then recorded and used for reading instruction, as in other language-experience activities. The information reading technique, according to Schneiderman, provides an added dimension to language experience in that it "gives the learner new information as well as experiences with the usual language and sentence structure of written material through active listening to orally presented material" (p. 17).

In its focus on the interests and needs of individual learners, the language-experience approach offers a number of desirable features to beginning adult readers. When he creates his own reading matter, the adult student has an added personal investment in his learning. Furthermore, he is able to focus on words and phrases of particular importance to him in his life and work. Failure of students to perceive such direct relationships between tasks expected of them in the classroom and those they must perform in their daily lives has caused the downfall of many adult education programs.

One other aspect of the language-experience approach seems especially important for adult learners. This approach emphasizes the relationship between speaking and reading as parallel language processes. The adult student has a fully developed spoken language and usually an advanced vocabulary, in comparison with his reading ability. In enabling the beginning reader to focus directly on the printed versions of his spoken words, the language-experience approach affords maximum opportunity for the adult to apply his overall language competence to his beginning reading efforts.

# The Assisted Reading Approach

"Assisted reading" (Hoskisson and Krohm, 1974), a simple approach to teaching beginning reading, is based on the assumption that the process of learning to read is comparable to learning to speak. Both processes, according to Smith (1971), are learned to a much greater extent than they are taught. While it is certainly true, according to this rationale, that a person who is learning to read or to speak may profit from his exposure to more experienced resource persons, that which he must learn *implicitly* far exceeds that which he can be *explicitly* taught. This is perhaps more obvious in learning to speak, as outlined below.

## Learning to Speak

Except by providing the labels for certain objects and actions which interest him, no one really teaches a child to speak. Parents and other experienced speakers subject the child continually to expressions of verbal language, not in isolated sounds and words but in fluent sentences, expressed in full-flowing syntax. After a series of progressively more successful efforts to produce sentences of his own, and encouragement from experienced speakers, a child, almost without exception, and at a very young age, achieves impressive facility with spoken language. The child does this from self-motivation and without any appreciable explicit knowledge of grammatical and linguistic rules for word and sentence construction. The assisted reading technique is based on the assumption that reading can be learned in a parallel and similar fashion.

## Stages and Content

There are basically three stages in the assisted reading process. In the first stage, as the beginning reader observes, an experienced reader moves his finger from word to word across a printed page and reads aloud, pronouncing the words in meaningful phrases and sentences. The beginning reader repeats the words as they are pointed to again. This cycle continues, with the beginning reader repeating a few words, after the experienced reader, in meaningful phrases, while carefully observing word-sound correspondences as they appear and sound in normal sentence syntax. Gradually, the beginning reader moves into the second stage of the assisted reading process; he recognizes and vocalizes some of the words himself, before they are supplied by the experienced reader. In the third stage of assisted reading, the beginning reader takes full initiative, pronouncing all the words he can, while only those words he does not know are supplied by his "assistant."

Assisted reading is particularly effective when used in combination with the language-experience approach to reading instruction. This is accomplished by encouraging the reader to provide his own printed matter (in his own vocabulary and syntax) through dictation.

A variety of materials is used in assisted reading in order to expose the learner to a wide breadth of written language. At the same time, however, the same materials are repeated frequently in order to reinforce learning and increase reader confidence. As a result, the learner's level of independence may fluctuate, depending upon the content.

The beginning adult reader should be encouraged to select reading matter of personal interest or relevance to his work. Using such material, he is more highly motivated and has the background information and vocabulary to make fluency more readily attainable. These advantages may be even more pronounced when assisted reading is focused on the printed version of the learner's spoken language. In this case, the learner not only has ample background information and familiarity with the vocabulary and syntax in the printed message but is ideally equipped to transfer to reading the fluency he has already achieved in speech. One of the older students in our reading clinic for illiterate university employees, a sixty-nine-year-old dining hall worker with no prior reading experience, dictated this passage:

> Mr. Henderson sent word for me and my other sister to come to work. So both of us got a job the same day. I come in here on the fifteenth of September, thirty years ago. I served on the lines and helped to feed the students.

Although this passage is much shorter than the typical assisted reading selection, it illustrates the fact that spoken English, especially that of adult illiterates, is often much different in syntax from passages that normally appear in print. Clearly, it is of significant advantage to the beginning reader to focus his efforts on syntax and vocabulary with which he is familiar.

## Extensions and Variations

The basic assisted reading instructional approach is amenable to a number of modifications which may be helpful to the beginning reader at various points in his instructional program. Assisted reading may be focused upon high-interest material that the student has previously memorized or with which he is familiar (if he has not dictated it himself). Since many adult illiterates are intent upon learning to read the Bible, we have used biblical passages for this purpose, trying to focus on selections which are reasonably short, generally familiar, and have fairly conventional syntax. As mentioned previously, memorization of text is an asset to the beginning reader in the earliest stages of his development. The effort to associate words in print with those spoken in meaningful phrases is greatly facilitated if the reader is able to anticipate what is coming.

As a variation in the mechanics of the assisted reading technique, the instructor and student may occasionally begin with the student pointing at words and the instructor identifying them. In addition to the fact that it offers a change of pace from the standard procedure, this modification is useful in helping students grasp the basic idea of "between word divisions" —the fact that one "clump of letters" corresponds to one spoken word.

An extension of assisted reading which may be employed, once beginning readers become familiar with the basic technique, is to combine it with the *cloze* procedure as an instructional (rather than evaluative) tool. The cloze procedure, as employed in reading-instructional and diagnostic circles, usually involves the omission of every fifth word in a passage (first and last sentences remain intact). The student who is able to comprehend a passage is able to fill in many of the missing words (or their synonyms) as a result of the meaning he derives from the remainder of the text.

The cloze procedure is ordinarily used to test the ability of readers to understand a particular selection (or to determine if the selection is appropriate for the readers). When used in conjunction with assisted reading, the cloze procedure is employed somewhat differently and its mechanics are modified accordingly. Instead of focusing on passages with every fifth word omitted, the beginning reader may be presented with passages in which only selected key words are missing (usually nouns or modifiers which are highly predictable). As the assistant reads aloud, the student supplies the missing word (represented by a blank) or an alternative which makes sense in the context. To acclimate the student to this procedure, he may first be exposed to passages which offer him a choice of three alternatives for each blank, such as "I had an earache. I went to the _____ (movies, doctor, bowling)." In this case, all three responses differ in appropriateness. The response *movies* is syntactically, but not semantically, acceptable; *bowling* is neither syntactically nor semantically acceptable. Any consistency of response of this latter type would suggest that the student has either no sense of the language or of the meaning he is attempting to comprehend.

The cloze procedure, when used as described above, accomplishes several purposes, all consistent with the assisted reading rationale. In the first place, the assisted reading/modified cloze procedure highlights the fact that reading is a matter of making sense of print, not simply of decoding words. The beginning reader must be encouraged to use context to predict what words (and meanings) might appear at particular points in print, based upon the meaning and syntax which precede them. Furthermore, the assisted reading/modified cloze procedure serves to impress upon the beginning reader that effective reading-for-meaning does not ordinarily depend upon the precise decoding of every individual word. On the contrary, too much attention to decoding individual words may cause the reader to lose meaning altogether.

As noted previously, beginning readers need to be convinced that they have read successfully when they have acquired the information they are seeking, whether or not they are able to identify every printed word. Similarly, when reading for recreation, as opposed to seeking specific information, the reader has been successful when he understands the overall content.

## Rationale

As discussed earlier, no one knows exactly what subskills must be mastered for successful speaking or reading. What we *do* know is that both of these processes have been mastered by motivated learners upon repeated exposure to a full language context. In reading, this requires that word-symbol correspondences be identified for the beginner in the flow of natural written syntax until he acquires the ability to do this himself.

The crucial assumption in assisted reading is that the key element in all language processes is fluency, and this must not be destroyed. Just as the child learns to speak from repeated exposure to a full context of oral language, the beginning reader learns from repeated interaction with the syntactically complete printed message. At no time, even in the third stage of the assisted reading process, is the reader asked to sound out words or to focus on separate word elements; he is simply supplied with words he does not know. In this manner, the fluency of reading as a language process is preserved.

Although study of reading subskills is not undertaken in the assisted reading approach, teachers have noticed that the reader becomes adept at making and applying phonics generalizations of his own. For example, a five-year-old, who had been taught by assisted reading, tested at high second grade level in decoding skills before he entered school — without having received phonics instruction (Hoskisson, 1974). At the same time, although no emphasis is placed upon identification of sight words, assisted reading provides a means by which the student may learn many words incidentally, without a concerted effort to memorize them.

Assisted reading occurs in a supportive and nonthreatening teaching-learning environment. Each beginning reader proceeds through the three stages at his own pace. Since no expectations are placed on the learner, other than repeating words after his "assistant," there are no failures and no occasion for frustration; the learner gets an immediate sense that he is reading. This is particularly important for the adult remedial reader's delicate self-concept.

One drawback in the assisted reading instructional approach, from the teacher's point of view, is the difficulty of serving all learners adequately on an individual basis. This difficulty can be resolved in various ways. Teachers may read selections onto tapes, allowing gaps for students to repeat phrases. On occasion, assisted reading may be conducted on a group basis if material can be located whose content is appropriate for a number of readers. This occurs most often in instances where a number of learners have common job-related interests, such as a group of industry employees interested in reading safety regulations.

The assisted reading approach offers a special incentive to students to locate "assistants" of their own and to continue their learning outside the classroom.

# Chapter 6

# Word Identification (Phase II)

In our program we have tried to recognize the life circumstances of the adult learner, as well as the learning situations typical of many adult classes. Also, we have tried to recognize the time constraints faced by adult-literacy students and teachers. Because of these conditions, we are faced with certain tradeoffs. We could try to teach more reading skills or to teach those in our organization in greater depth. Instead, our emphasis has been on the adult illiterate's exposure to the tools necessary to contend with the basic reading demands of his environment; we have tried to avoid overwhelming him with an oversupply of complicated rules and exercises. Many prepackaged reading programs contain an abundance of such "frills" — largely, we think, because they were designed for school children in instructional programs where time is not at a premium. As a rule, these programs are not geared to the "survival skills" of the adult functional illiterate.

The problem with the mass of available basal and programmed materials for teaching word-identification skills is not that these materials do not emphasize the "right" skills or the "right" teaching methods, but that they emphasize too many skills and methods. In developing a program for word identification, our role has been to pick and choose — to select the skills and methods most consistent with our beliefs about how reading is learned, coupled with our best insight into the unique nature of the adult illiterate. As a consequence, our program is not original (except perhaps in the manner in which it combines and sequences the ideas of others), but it is designed to give time-conscious adult students the most for their learning

The coauthor of this chapter is Jeanne H. Ford.

efforts and activities. In our work we have referred frequently to three contemporary reading texts: Johnson and Pearson's *Teaching Reading Vocabulary* (1977), Cunningham, Arthur, and Cunningham's *Classroom Reading Instruction K–5* (1977), and Spache and Spache's *Reading in the Elementary School* (1977).

In the context of our continuum of reading development, it seems appropriate to begin word-identification instruction only after the student has gained substantial exposure to printed language as a whole. Refinement of decoding skills should be taught only after the learner has attained a general knowledge of how reading "works." The student needs orientation to the printed page, as well as a general purpose for reading ("to receive a message from the author"), before he can understand when and where to utilize specific word-identification skills.

It must be constantly borne in mind, though, that word-identification skills are merely means to an end, not ends in themselves. In other words, we don't want to lose sight of the forest for the trees. To avoid the problem, language-experience and assisted reading should be continued while word-identification skills are taught, so that students may continue to "read" while learning to refine these skills. By tying word-identification skills together with the more global aspects of reading, students are more apt to see the benefit of refining these skills.

With these factors in mind, we have organized a sequence for teaching word-identification skills which is based on the notion that learning should move from the known to the unknown. We have attempted to order these skills from those of a more generalized nature to those of a more specific nature. An organization of instruction based upon these principles is best calculated to minimize abstraction and confusion for the insecure and time-conscious adult illiterate.

In keeping with this rationale, the following is an outline of the general types of word-identification skills that we feel should be included in teaching adults to read.

1.  Contextual clues
    a)  Pictorial and graphic
    b)  Syntactic
    c)  Semantic
2.  Sight words
3.  Phonics
    a)  Initiation of letter-sound correspondences
    b)  Rhyming words and phonics
    c)  Consonant plus context
    d)  Rule derivation
4.  Structural analysis
    a)  Prefixes and suffixes
    b)  Syllabication

The following discussion is not meant to be an exhaustive review of how to teach skills in these areas; rather, we hope to help teachers gain some understanding of what each skill entails, with examples of how each can be taught. Based upon this framework, teachers of adults can devise supplementary activities as needed or locate them in skill-building texts such as those used in basal and programmed materials.

# Contextual Clues

The first type of word-identification skill that we think important for the reader is the contextual clue. A contextual clue is basically a clue to word identification which is derived from the environment in which a word appears. In other words, comprehension aids such as the pictures on the page, the meanings and parts of speech of surrounding words, and definitional footnotes can help in identifying unknown words in that they cause the reader to focus on the overall meaning of the text. The reader may thus draw upon his background experience and knowledge and thereby make more accurate hypotheses as to the meaning and identification of individual words.

There are three types of contextual clues which we feel should be taught explicitly to adult remedial readers: pictorial and graphic, syntactic, and semantic. In keeping with our beliefs about how people learn, our discussion of these clues progresses from those which are more generalized to those which are more specific.

## Pictorial and Graphic Clues

The reader can gain much information about the printed page from pictures, graphs, charts, etc., that are given in the text. Teachers can encourage the use of such clues by asking students to speculate on the meaning of a particular passage or word before reading. When focusing upon leading questions, based upon pictorial and graphic clues, the student can learn much from a page before he even begins to look at the words.

## Syntactic Clues

The syntactic clue to word identification is derived from the grammatical structure of the context in which a word appears. The English language is known as a *positional* language because of the importance of word order in communicating meaning. Certain parts of speech are appropriate in particular position in a sentence while others are not. Consider the following examples:

THE _____ FELL OFF THE TABLE.

WE _____ TO THE STORE.

HE LIVES IN THE _____ HOUSE.

Clearly, the three missing words must be a noun, a verb, and an adjective respectively. There are no other possibilities. While syntactic clues alone are not sufficient for word identification, they are helpful in the elimination of unlikely alternatives. Syntactic clues are most effectively employed in conjunction with other approaches to word identification.

The syntactic clue, then, is another type of clue from the context of the print, based primarily in sentence structure and parts of speech of surrounding words. The reader calls upon his intrinsic knowledge of language to assist him in making hypotheses concerning unknown words.

One can encourage students to use this type of clue through cloze activities, in which they are given sentences with words (usually every fifth) deleted and asked to provide a word that "makes sense" according to the rules of the language. Also (as described earlier), during language-experience and assisted reading activities, one can delete words from a new passage and ask students to fill in the blanks. These activities encourage students to call upon their knowledge of oral language as an aid to learning printed language.

## Semantic Clues

When using semantic clues, the student examines the *meaning* of the words preceding and following a word in order to hypothesize what that word might be. Again, the cloze procedure provides the best practice in using this type of clue. Cloze activities should consist initially of oral exercises; later, they should be used in conjunction with assisted reading. Finally, the student should focus upon cloze activities independently. Although the cloze procedure most commonly involves deletion of every fifth word (though the first and the last sentence of a passage are intact), the teacher may vary these activities by eliminating fewer words or particular parts of speech.

# Sight Words

Identification of sight words out of context is a more specialized skill for beginning readers than the use of contextual clues, since they are unable to use their background experience and prior knowledge of language to the same extent. At the same time, sight-word identification is not as highly specialized as phonics and structural analysis, which draw the illiterate adult even further into areas of print with which he is unfamiliar.

Most sight words should come from the student's activities in language-experience and assisted reading. Students should be given activities that facilitate word identification by means of picture association, meaningful associations of known words (such as *bacon and eggs*), and practice in clas- sification. For example, Cunningham, Arthur, and Cunningham (1977) describe an activity in which the student cuts out pictures from magazines, pastes them on index cards, and dictates the word he associates with each picture (which is then written on the opposite side of the index card). Students can practice looking at the words printed on the cards and testing their responses by looking at the associated pictures. Also, the teacher can use these sight words by placing them in sentences with other known words, then rearranging the words into new sentences; for example: "A dog was running up the street" to "Running up the street was a dog."

Students should also receive sight training pertaining to words most frequently used in print. The Dolch (1942) basic sight vocabulary is a helpful tool for this purpose. We suggest that the student be introduced to approximately four or five words from this list per class session. These should be presented first in the context of sentences. Flash-card games can then be used for additional reinforcement — as well as having the student identify the words in new sentences. Reinforcement should continue in subsequent class sessions to ensure that each word is firmly planted in the student's memory.

# Phonics

Needless to say, phonics is one of the most highly specialized skills required of most beginning readers. Appropriate phonics training can provide students with word-identification skills that enable them to become more independent readers. Our discussion of phonics will be divided into two subsections: the rationale for our "modified" phonics program and the program itself.

## Rationale for a Modified Phonics Program

There are many approaches to teaching phonics, each of which makes different demands on students' time and abilities to think abstractly. Some programs require students to learn one or more sound associations with all the letters of the alphabet and then string the sounds together to form words. Others require students to memorize various rules in order to "crack the code." The number of such phonics generalizations is almost limitless in some of these programs, and the learner is called upon to know when and where to use each generalization.

When one considers the time constraints on the adult illiterate in the classroom, however, and the necessity that he experience at least *some* immediate success, it is apparent that the teacher must set criteria for choosing which "rules" and generalizations are most crucial for independent reading. If such criteria are not set, the learner may be required to learn too many rules. Inevitably, the more rules a beginning reader is required to learn, the less the facility with which he will be able to employ any individual rule and the more confused he is likely to become. It is thus incumbent upon the teacher to select for instruction only those rules which are reasonably dependable (i.e., for which exceptions are minimal) and reasonably easy to learn and to apply. In order to adopt reasonably valid criteria for selecting what rules to teach in view of these concerns, the teacher can profit from specialized information pertaining to these issues.

Table 5 summarizes the findings of three independent researchers as to the utility of thirty-seven phonetic generalizations. Although these researchers may disagree somewhat on whether certain instances of particular letter combinations constitute conformity or exceptions to a particular rule, it is apparent that students are often taught many rules that are only minimally efficient. The more rules the illiterate must struggle to learn, the more likely that his facility with those rules which are the most dependable will diminish. Also, the chances are that he will struggle to learn rules with high proportions of exceptions, which may prove as much a hindrance as an asset in his early efforts to decode and make sense of print.

The learning of phonics can be a much more difficult undertaking for the beginning reader than is generally supposed. Also, use of phonics to the exclusion of other means of teaching and learning reading may be highly impractical. Frank Smith (1973) reports and comments upon one "systematic effort" to "construct a workable set of phonics rules for English" (p. 87). That effort, by researchers Bierdiansky, Cronnell, and Koehler (1969), identified distinct sound-symbol correspondences for 6,092 one- and two-syllable words "in the comprehension vocabularies of six to nine year old children" (p. 88). The results are recorded in table 6 (Smith's table 1).

Smith (1973) comments as follows:

> The researchers discovered that their 6,000 words involved 211 distinct spelling-sound "correspondences"—this does not mean that 211 different sounds were represented, but that the phonemes that did occur were represented by a total of 211 different spellings (obviously, some of the grapheme units were related to more than one sound). The results are summarized in Table 1 [table 6]. Eighty-three of the correspondences involved consonant grapheme units, and 128 involved vowel grapheme units, including no fewer than 79 that were associated with the six "primary" single-letter vowels, a, e, i, o, u, y. In other words, there was a total of 79 different ways in which the single vowels could be pronounced. Of the 211 correspondences, 45 were clusters of exceptions, about half involving vowels and half consonants. The exclusion of 45 correspondences from the "rules" meant that nearly ten percent of the 6,092 words had to be regarded as "exceptions."

TABLE 5. UTILITY OF PHONICS GENERALIZATIONS

| | PERCENT OF UTILITY | | |
|---|---|---|---|
| VOWEL PRINCIPLES | CLYMER[a] | EMANS[b] | BAILEY[c] |
| 1. When y is the final letter in a word, it usually has a vowel sound. | 84 | 98 | 89 |
| 2. If the only vowel letter is at the end of a word, the letter usually stands for a long sound. | 74 | 33 | 76 |
| 3. When there is one e in a word that ends in a consonant, the e usually has a short sound. | 76 | 83 | 92 |
| 4. When a vowel is in the middle of a one-syllable word, ending in a consonant, the vowel is short. | 62 | 73 | 71 |
| 5. When there are two vowels, one of which is final e, the first vowel is long and the e is silent. | 63 | 63 | 57 |
| 6. When words end with silent e, the preceding a or i is long. | 60 | 48 | 50 |
| 7. One vowel letter in an accented syllable has its short sound. | 61 | 64 | 65 |
| 8. In many two- and three-syllable words, the final e lengthens the vowel in the last syllable. | 46 | 42 | 46 |
| 9. The letter a has the same sound (o) when followed by l, w, and u. | 48 | 24 | 34 |
| 10. When a follows w in a word, it usually has the sound of a in was. | 32 | 28 | 22 |
| 11. When y is used as a vowel in words, it sometimes has the sound of long i. | 15 | 4 | 11 |
| 12. When y or ey is seen in the last syllable that is not accented, the long sound of e is heard. | 0 | 1 | 0 |

| VOWEL DIGRAPHS | CLYMER[a] | EMANS[b] | BAILEY[c] |
|---|---|---|---|
| 13. When the letters oa are together in a word, o always gives its long sound and the a is silent. | 97 | 86 | 95 |
| 14. Words having double e usually have the long e sound. | 98 | 100 | 87 |
| 15. In ay the y is silent and gives a its long sound. | 78 | 100 | 88 |
| 16. When ea comes together in a word, the first letter is long, the second silent. | 66 | 62 | 55 |
| 17. The first vowel is usually long, the second silent, in the digraphs ai, ea, oa, ui. | 66 | 58 | 60 |
| 18. When there are two vowels side by side, the long sound of the first one is heard and the second is usually silent. | 45 | 18 | 34 |
| 19. W is sometimes a vowel and follows the vowel digraph rule. | 40 | 31 | 33 |
| 20. In the phonogram ie, the i is silent and the e has a long sound. | 17 | 23 | 31 |

TABLE 5. (Continued)

| VOWEL DIPHTHONGS | CLYMER[a] | EMANS[b] | BAILEY[c] |
|---|---|---|---|
| 21. The two letters ow make the long o sound. | 59 | 50 | 55 |
| 22. When e is followed by w, the vowel sound is the same as represented by oo. | 35 | 14 | 40 |

| VOWELS WITH R | CLYMER[a] | EMANS[b] | BAILEY[c] |
|---|---|---|---|
| 23. The r gives the preceding vowel a sound that is neither long nor short. | 78 | 82 | 86 |
| 24. When a is followed by r and final e, we expect to hear the sound heard in *care*. | 90 | 100 | 96 |

| CONSONANTS | CLYMER[a] | EMANS[b] | BAILEY[c] |
|---|---|---|---|
| 25. When c and h are next to each other, they make only one sound. | 100 | 100 | 100 |
| 26. When the letter c is followed by o or a, the sound of k is likely to be heard. | 100 | 100 | 100 |
| 27. When ght is seen in a word, gh is silent. | 100 | 100 | 100 |
| 28. When a word begins with kn, the k is silent. | 100 | 100 | 100 |
| 29. When a word begins with wr, the w is silent. | 100 | 100 | 100 |
| 30. When a word ends in ck, it has the same sound as in look. | 100 | 100 | 100 |
| 31. When two of the same consonants are side by side, only one is heard. | 99 | 91 | 98 |
| 32. When c is followed by e or i, the sound of s is likely to be heard. | 96 | 90 | 92 |
| 33. Ch is usually pronounced as it is in *kitchen*, *catch*, and *chair*, not like sh. | 95 | 67 | 87 |
| 34. The letter g often has a sound similar to that of j in *jump* when it precedes the letter i or e. | 64 | 80 | 78 |

| PHONOGRAMS | CLYMER[a] | EMANS[b] | BAILEY[c] |
|---|---|---|---|
| 35. When the letter i is followed by the letters gh, the i usually stands for its long sound, and the gh is silent. | 71 | 100 | 71 |
| 36. When ture is the final syllable in a word, it is unaccented. | 100 | 100 | 95 |
| 37. When tion is the final syllable in a word, it is unaccented. | 100 | 100 | 100 |

*Source:* George Spache and Evelyn Spache, *Reading in the Elementary School* (Boston: Allyn and Bacon, 1977), pp. 375–77. Copyright 1977 by Allyn and Bacon, Inc. Reprinted by permission.
Data are from the following sources:

[a]T. Clymer, "The Utility of Phonic Generalizations in the Primary Grades," *Reading Teacher*, 16: 252-58.
[b]R. Emans, "The Usefulness of Phonic Generalizations above the Primary Grades," *Reading Teacher*, 20: 419-25.
[c]M. H. Bailey, "The Utility of Phonic Generalizations in Grades One through Six," *Reading Teacher*, 20: 413-18.

The pronunciation of the remaining words was accounted for by a grand total of 166 rules! Sixty of these rules were concerned with the pronunciation of consonants (which are generally thought to have fairly "regular" pronunciations) and 106 with single or complex vowels.   [p. 88]

It is rarely true, as Smith acknowledges, that a reader is in "absolute doubt about what a word might be" and thus forced to rely on phonics entirely. At the same time, it must be recognized that phonics can provide only clues to sound and word recognition. Even if a novice reader were to memorize 166 rules—a staggering expectation, especially for the time-conscious and apprehensive adult illiterate—he would often be uncertain what rule (or exception) applies to a given situation. In another source, for example, Smith (1971) poses the question of how many different ways the letters *ho* may be pronounced at the beginning of a word. In a list of possibilities, he suggests "hot, hoot, hook, hour, honest, house, hope, honey, hoist" (p. 168).

TABLE 6. SPELLING-SOUND CORRESPONDENCES AMONG 6,092 ONE-AND TWO-SYLLABLE WORDS IN VOCABULARIES OF NINE-YEAR-OLD CHILDREN

|  | CONSONANTS | PRIMARY VOWELS | SECONDARY VOWELS | TOTAL |
|---|---|---|---|---|
| Spelling-sound correspondences | 83 | 79 | 49 | 211 |
| "Rules" | 60 | 73 | 33 | 166 |
| "Exceptions" | 23 | 6 | 16 | 45 |
| Grapheme units in rules | 44 | 6 | 19 | 69 |

Source: *Understanding Reading: A Psychological Analysis of Reading and Learning to Read* by Frank Smith. Copyright ©1971 by Holt, Rinehart and Winston, Inc. Reprinted by permission of Holt, Rinehart and Winston.

The fact is that lists of phonics rules are constructed by experienced readers according to their own logic regarding what beginners need to learn. Experienced readers are prone to overlook many obstacles which confront beginning readers in such dilemmas as the *ho* problem. To a person who can already read (and who already knows most of the words and the context), there is little difficulty in determining what rule applies in a particular instance. For the novice, on the other hand, uncertainty on this issue often complicates an already abstract and complicated learning process.

In summary, any teacher of reading must carefully decide how phonics will be taught to beginning readers in terms of the dependability of specific generalizations (rules) and the feasibility of their applications. For the adult illiterate, the situation is even more complicated. School usually meets only a few hours a week; so time for learning numerous complicated rules is not often available.

In view of the preceding concerns, we advocate a modified phonics program, much of which we borrow from Cunningham, Arthur, and Cunningham (1977), in which only selected letter-sound correspondences are taught in conjunction with rhyming words. This procedure reduces abstraction for the novice reader and avoids the explicit teaching of potentially confusing phonics generalizations until the student has begun to understand the fundamentals of sound-symbol correspondence in word attack.

## Modified Phonics Instructional Program

**Initiation of Letter-Sound Correspondences.** The beginning of phonics training for adult remedial readers should come as a natural extension to sight-word training. With a list of the student's sight words, the teacher guides the student in identifying similarities and differences among the words' beginning letters and in associating initial consonants and their sounds. (Consonants are taught before vowels because their sounds are generally more consistent.) Students may practice initial consonant letter-sound association by finding pictures of objects in magazines whose names start with the consonants that are being studied. As they become familiar with these associations, students may be presented with oral and written exercises in which they are asked to provide the first letters of words which are read to them or which appear in print, with the first letters deleted.

This basic procedure for teaching letter-sound correspondences for initial consonants can be extended for teaching initial blends, initial digraphs, final consonants, and final blends and digraphs as well. In deciding what consonants to teach, we suggest that the teacher use the format listed below. (This format is based on portions of a scheme provided by Spache and Spache [1977].)

Simple consonants: *b, p, m, w, h, d, t, n,* hard *g* (gate), *k,* hard *c* (cake), *y* (yet), *f* (for)

More difficult consonants: *v, l, z* (zoo), *s* (sat), *r, c* (cent), *q* (kw), *x* (ks), *j, g* (engine), *s* (as)

Consonant blends and digraphs: *ck, ng, th* (the), *zh, sh, th* (thin), *wh, ch*

Simple consonants with *l, r, p,* or *t: bl, pl, gr, br, sp, st, tr, thr, str, spl, scr,* and others as they appear (pp. 380–81)

Consistent with the purposes and the design of our program, the teacher should first instruct the students in learning the simple and more difficult consonants in the initial positions of words. Once this is accomplished, instruction should begin on initial blends and digraphs, followed by training in final consonants, blends, and digraphs, respectively. Training in vowel sounds occurs as students are instructed in "consonant substitution" exercises, as described in the next section.

**Rhyming Words and Phonics.** In conjunction with letter-sound correspondences, our phonics program focuses upon rhyming words. We adopted this approach from a strategy described by Cunningham, Arthur, and Cunningham (1977) in which students learn to identify unknown words through use of "key word" sets.

As a beginning step in this strategy, students need to become familiar with the basic concept of rhyming words. This may be accomplished by exposing them to these words in the contexts of songs, poems, and colloquial sayings. By reading rhyming words in these contexts, students will acquire their orientation to this concept in a true "language experience" fashion. The teacher should draw attention to the words that rhyme — pointing out similarities and differences in these words' auditory and written forms. Most importantly, the students should be led to discover that the endings of rhyming words are generally spelled and sound alike and that usually the only differences in these words occur at the beginning.

The essence of the rhyming words approach to phonics skills is "consonant substitution." In consonant substitution exercises, a word is written on the board and other rhyming words are generated by substituting various consonants in place of the original initial consonant. Once students understand word similarities and differences as revealed in this way, they are taught to use a list of "key words" (sight words used as models in identifying words) in conjunction with their knowledge of letter-sound correspondences and of the rhyming concept for word identification. A typical lesson of this type is described by Cunningham, Arthur, and Cunningham (1977) as follows:

> Currently each child [student] has five cards on which I have written the words *and, run, man,* and *boy.* I write a word on the board which ends like and rhymes with one of these five words on their cards. They must then sort through their five cards and find the "look-alike" word. At a signal from me, all children [students] show their look-alike word. We talk about where the words are alike (at the end) and where they're different (at the beginning) and what they will probably do (rhyme). Then someone volunteers to come up to the board, match his or her word to mine, and pronounce both words. In this way the children [students] are having to search for the model, but from a tangible limited store of words. When the children [students] show facility at matching these five words, I will add two more and then two more until eventually they have about fifteen words. These fifteen words will all be words that have many words which rhyme with them, and which the children [students] recognize as sight words. [p. 75]

From such training the student learns a great deal about vowels' letter-sound relationships without becoming bogged down with a great many rules and their exceptions. Essentially, the student learns to build on what he already knows—a natural learning situation.

For the core of "key words," we suggest that the teacher concentrate on using those whose endings are frequently seen in print. Spache and Spache (1977) suggests a list of phonograms that may be helpful in identifying such words.

Phonograms: ail, ain, all, and, ate, ay, con, eep, ell, en, ent, er, est, ick, ight, ill, in, ing, ock, ter, tion
Alternates—ake, ide, ile, ine, it, ite, le, re, ble. [p. 381]

As students increase their list of key words, as well as learn new letter-sound correspondences for different positions in a word, ability to decipher unknown words multiplies rapidly and thereby increases reading independence. In this manner, the learner's newly acquired phonics skills provide immediate payoff and both help and encourage his continued reading development.

This knowledge of rhyming words and letter-sound correspondences is an important aspect of our phonics program. Students learn the less abstract letter-sound correspondences (initial consonants, etc.) from direct instruction. However, the more abstract vowel-sound correspondences are learned in the context of letter patterns. In this manner, word identification through phonics is maintained on a level that emphasizes knowledge of words in conjunction with letter-sound correspondences. That is in contrast to emphasis on an abstract process of "stringing sounds together" that can encourage students to ignore other aspects of word identification, such as sight recognition and structural analysis.

**Consonant plus Context.** Another strategy described by Cunningham, Arthur, and Cunningham (1977), the "consonant plus context" strategy, is also a most useful tool in getting students to apply their phonics knowledge in general reading. This strategy emphasizes use of the unknown word's context in a particular passage, along with the word's initial letter-sound, to aid the student in word identification. This is a particularly helpful way to train students in using several types of word-identification clues together as they read passages of text.

The following is a passage from Cunningham, Arthur, and Cunningham (1977) that describes a particular teacher's use of this consonant-plus-context strategy.

Once they [the students] have learned some consonant letter-sound associations, I teach them to use those associations and the context to figure out unknown words. I use the overhead projector and let them help me read a sentence in which one word is covered up. We say *blank* when we come to that word. Then they guess all the words that might go in that blank and I make a list of these guesses on the board. I uncover the first letter of the unknown word. We then decide which words on the board are now impossible and erase them. Sometimes we add more words which begin with the uncovered letter and they guess which one they think it might be and explain why they think this. We uncover the word and discover what the word is. In this way, the children [students] learn that the context will somewhat limit the possibilities for an unknown word and the first letter will limit it even more. These exercises are fun and I am beginning to see the children [students] use these context-plus-consonant clues in their reading.   [p. 77]

Using the consonant-plus-context strategy for word identification, then, should provide the learner with practice in a strategy that is used by fluent readers. In turn, it should help remedial students on their way to becoming fluent readers themselves.

**Rule Derivation.** We have described two strategies for phonics training that emphasize the use of phonics in conjunction with other word-identification skills. At this point in his experience with word-identification skills, however, the student may be ready to study *selected* phonics generalizations, without the support of such aids as rhyming words and context clues. It is still necessary, of course, that the teacher be careful to select only rules of maximum dependability and utility. Spache and Spache (1977) suggest that the following meet this criteria.

*Consonants*
1.  When c is frequently followed by e, i, or y, it has the sound of s, as in race, city, fancy.
2.  Otherwise, c has the sound of k, as in come, attic.
3.  G followed by e, i, or y sounds soft like j, as in gem.
4.  Otherwise, g sounds hard, as in gone.
5.  When c and h are next to each other, they make only one sound.
6.  Ch is usually pronounced as it is in kitchen, not like sh (in machine).
7.  When a word ends in ck, it has the same last sound, as in look.
8.  When two of the same consonants are side by side, only one is heard, as in butter.
9.  Sometimes s has the sound of z, as in raisin, music.
10.  The letter x has the sounds of ks or k and s, as in box, taxi.

*Vowels*
11.  When a consonant and y are the last letters in a one-syllable word, the y has the long i sound, as in cry, by. In longer words the y has the lone e sound, as in baby.
12.  The r gives the preceding vowel a sound that is neither long nor short, as in car, far, fur, fir. The letters l and w have the same effect.

*Vowel Digraphs and Diphthongs*
13.  The first vowel is usually long and the second silent in oa, ay, ai, and ee, as in boat, say, gain, feed.

14. In ea the first letter may be long and the second silent, or it may have the short e sound, as in bread.

15. Ou has two sounds: one is the long sound of o; the other is the ou sound, as in own or cow.

16. These double vowels blend into a single sound: au, aw, oi, oy, as in auto, awful, coin, boy.

17. The combination ou has a schwa sound, as in vigorous, or a sound as in out.

18. The combination oo has two sounds, as in moon and as in wood. [pp. 382-83]

If the teacher decides to focus upon these or other phonics generalizations, we suggest that they be taught inductively, by having the student(s) generate the rules employed. We will illustrate this procedure with regard to the Spaches' rule 3 (above), though it is equally appropriate for most phonics concepts. In the case of rule 3, the teacher might write twelve words on the blackboard, beginning with *g*, as follows:

| | | |
|---|---|---|
| GIANT | GEM | GERM |
| GYP | GOAL | GYM |
| GOAT | GATE | GIRAFFE |
| GAME | GONE | GLAD |

He would then ask that these words be read aloud. Any words that are unfamiliar to the students he reads himself. When the list has been read aloud several times, the teacher asks what students can tell him about the sound of *g* in these words. After some guided experimentation, students will conclude that two basic sounds are being illustrated (hard and soft sounds of *g*) and, with the teacher's help, inductively derive a rule which can be recorded in the following form:

WHEN G IS FOLLOWED BY *I, E,* OR *Y,* IT FREQUENTLY MAKES THE SOUND
THAT *J* MAKES; OTHERWISE IT MAKES THE SOUND WE HEAR IN *GO.*

In a sense, of course, students are directed to a conclusion they must accept on faith or because of their confidence in the teacher's knowledge. The twelve words selected for this exercise do not *prove* any truths about the language as a whole. The teacher should acknowledge that the rule does not always apply and should suggest some exceptions (particularly, in this case, a number of *gi* words, such as *give* and *girl*).

Despite the lack of perfection in most phonics generalizations, we have found that when adult students, even under somewhat artificial conditions, are led to derive a limited number of "rules" themselves, they frequently retain and apply them more effectively.

## Structural Analysis

Structural analysis can be described as that set of procedures which readers use to examine meaningful elements within words. Again, we will emphasize only areas of structural analysis which we feel are most useful and necessary in view of the time constraints on remedial readers. The following discussion will therefore focus upon only two major issues: prefixes and suffixes, and syllabication.

## Prefixes and Suffixes

A working knowledge of prefixes and suffixes provides a valuable aid to word identification and comprehension. From a word-identification standpoint, students may be presented with a number of teacher-constructed exercises for this purpose. These may include, for example, having students produce words by combining affixes to root words or from a scrambled list of affixes and root words. Students may also be asked to separate affixes from root words or to locate words containing affixes in a particular text.

In terms of comprehension emphasis, several additional activities are suggested, including providing the student with (1) the meaning of an affix, with examples of its use, (2) practice in matching words containing affixes with appropriate pictorial representations, and (3) practice in matching such words with written definitions and examples.

In addition to selecting strategies for the teaching of affixes, teachers must, of course, make decisions about what prefixes and suffixes will be taught. The following list compiled by Deighton (cited in Johnson and Pearson, 1978) may be used in selecting affixes for instruction.

*Invariant Prefixes* (prefixes with one meaning)
apo-, circum-, equi-, extra-, intra-, intro-, mal-, mis-, non-, syn-

*Variant Prefixes* (prefixes with more than one meaning)
bi-, de-, fore-, in-, pre-, pro-, semi-, re-, un-

*Noun Suffixes* (suffixes which indicate parts of speech)
-ance, -ence, -ation, (-tion, -ion), -ism, -ment, -acity, -hood, -ness, -dom, -ery, -mony, -ty, -tude, -ship

*Noun Suffixes* (indicating agent)
-eer, -ess, -grapher, -ier, -ster, -ist, -stress, -trix

*Noun Suffixes* (with specific meanings)
-ana, -archy, -ard, -aster, -bility, -chrome, -cide, -ee, -fer, -fication, -gram, -graph, -graphy, -ics, -itis, -latry, -meter, -metry, -ology, -phore, -phobic, -ric, -scope, -scopy

*Invariant Adjective Suffixes*
-est, -ferous, -fic, -fold, -form, -genous, -scopic, -wards, -wise, -less, -able, -ible, -most, -like, -ous, -ose, -acious, -ful.

Johnson and Pearson (1978) suggest training in the following basic affixes in conjunction with those recommended by Deighton:

*Inflected Endings*
(1) Plural: -s, -es; (2) Comparison: -er, -est; (3) Tense: -ed, -ing, -s; and (4) Possessive: s, s'.

Ideally, the teacher should select words that contain these affixes directly from the students' own word banks and language-experience stories and from familiar texts. Another option, of course, is for the teacher to create new words for the student to work with by adding affixes to familiar root words already in the student's repertoire. Eventually, in any case, the student should be able to identify an increasing number of unfamiliar words based on his knowledge of this aspect of structural analysis. Having these skills should greatly increase the student's independence in word identification — and ultimately his reading ability in general.

## Syllabication

Teaching syllabication as another aspect of structural analysis will provide students with an additional tool that is useful in word identification. It must be stressed, however, that it is not the purpose of this training to insist that the student learn a specific set of rules for dividing words into syllables. Rather, the purpose is to provide the student with what Johnson and Pearson (1978) call a "set for syllabication." With this "set," students become aware of the process of dividing words into pronounceable (and sometimes meaningful) units and are helped to identify words according to these units. To establish this "set for syllabication," Johnson and Pearson (1978) suggest the following training:

A. Teach the concept of the syllable from an auditory point of view; have the children [students] clap out syllables with you as you say a multisyllable word. Later have them count syllables as you say a word.

B. Teach a general concept of a syllable from a graphic point of view. One rule that does seem appropriate is that a syllable needs a vowel.

C. Combine steps (a) and (b) above. Have the written form in front of the children [students] as they clap out or count out syllables.

D. Give practice in systematically pronouncing regular words.

| Wash | No |
| Washing | Novem |
| Washington | November |

You can do this as a chalkboard or as a tachistoscopic exercise. Notice that it emphasizes left to right attack and that it reinforces both the visual and the auditory notion of a syllable.

E. Highlight syllables in running text for oral (or silent) reading exercises by underlining them or putting dots between them. This works as a *process* practice technique.

F. In discussion and practice, emphasize the joint utilization of syllabication processes, context, and oral language in order to move from an approximation of an unknown word to its specification. Remember, phonics is only of use if the word is already within the child's [student's] oral/aural vocabulary. [p. 75]

Training in syllabication, then, should be taught mostly on a conceptual level, rather than as a set of rules for dividing words. As a result, we have chosen the modified training strategy described above as most appropriate for adult students.

In conclusion, we must reiterate that we have provided only a framework and rationale for selecting activities for teaching word-identification skills to adults. We devised this format with an eye to particular skills' usefulness to the adult, as well as to the cost required to learn them in terms of student time and effort. Our purpose has been to provide students with the word-identification skills they need most while requiring only the sacrifices they can afford.

# Chapter 7

# Reading to Learn
# (Phase III)

When the adult remedial reader reaches Phase III in our instructional design, he has achieved a substantial level of reading independence. Although the two points of emphasis are never totally separate, it is fair to say that at this point the learner is focusing more upon reading to learn than upon learning to read. In other words, he has progressed from one end of the learning continuum to the other. As the student is able to focus more completely upon the information presented in the text, the definition of reading changes somewhat in an instructional context. As opposed simply to the word-recognition and decoding emphasis reflected in the conceptualizations of reading stated in association with Phases I and II, the emphasis is now entirely on comprehension: the reader's effort to derive meaning from print.

This chapter focuses upon two activities: content-area reading and sustained silent reading (SSR). The term *activities* is perhaps more appropriate than *methods* since the emphasis is primarily upon what the learner does independently. Nonetheless, the teacher's efforts can affect the extent to which the student develops his abilities to derive meaning from print.

## Content Reading

As previously noted at several points, the adult functional illiterate does not approach reading instruction with the purpose of simply learning to read reading. He is motivated to learn to read particular content. It was, in fact, his frustration in being unable to read specific material (newspapers, job orders, letters from his children, etc.) which motivated him to seek reading assistance in the first place. Content is thus the ultimate goal of any adult remedial reader.

The term *content area* is widely employed in discussions of reading in high school subject matter classes. In these instances, it generally refers to the special difficulties imposed upon students attempting to read textbooks in specific academic areas, such as social studies or science. The use of the term in this book is somewhat different, focusing not upon academic subjects but upon specialized job and life-related adult reading needs. The point of emphasis then becomes: What can we do to enhance the reading abilities of adult students in their chosen areas of interest?

To a considerable extent, we have been addressing this problem from the beginning. In Phase I of our instructional design and in our separate discussions of the language-experience and assisted reading approaches we have emphasized the necessity of addressing individual student needs through careful selection of personally relevant materials. But now this focus becomes more specific. As the adult student approaches reading independence in Phase III, how can we facilitate his efforts to overcome the particular obstacles which confront him in the subject matter which he most wants or needs to read?

Since the reading purposes of adults are as diverse as their individual interests, it would be impossible to anticipate the unique difficulties imposed by all the content reading matter which interests them. We will attempt, instead, to describe a set of categories into which these obstacles may be organized, evaluated, and addressed in an instructional framework. The teacher must then decide the extent to which each category of potential difficulties is relevant to the instructional needs of the individual student in his efforts to read the specific content which he chooses. We will organize our discussion of potential reading difficulties in the content areas under the following broad topical headings: conceptual framework, sense of purpose, organizational mechanics, vocabulary, and writing styles.

Again, it is necessary to emphasize that not every student will need help and not all reading matter will impose difficulties in all (or perhaps any) of these areas. These headings simply present an organization of categories by which potential reading problems encountered by students in different content areas may be examined.

## Conceptual Framework

This category of potential reading difficulty is concerned with the extent of background experience with which the reader attacks particular content material. Does he have sufficient background to comprehend what he is reading? In Phases I and II of our instructional design we emphasized that the student should focus on material he could easily understand, because, at these points, we were primarily interested in helping him translate printed symbols into spoken words. We did not want to complicate the beginning student's task by imposing upon him content with which he is unfamiliar. On the contrary, we expected the fact that he was familiar with the content both to motivate his efforts and to help him read by enabling him to predict meaning and thereby to use content as a primary tool in word attack.

Now that the adult student is approaching reading independence, the situation is somewhat different. He is no longer reading aloud to an instructor or helper but reading silently. Although he may frequently elect to read material for which he has considerable background (often more than the teacher), this is not always the case; he may choose material for which he has little background. He may, in fact, even be able to identify most of the words in a selection without grasping its content. This problem is often observed among high school students in subject matter classes, who may read aloud flawlessly from a textbook without grasping its message. Youthful readers may have the same problem with fiction and/or philosophical writing. Consider the following passage from James Baldwin's *Nobody Knows My Name:*

> And even in icy Sweden, I found myself talking with a man whose endless questioning has given him himself, and who reminded me of black Baptist preachers. The questions which one asks oneself begin at last to illuminate the world, and become one's key to the experience of others. One can only face in others what one can face in oneself. On this confrontation depends the measure of our wisdom and compassion. This energy is all that one finds in the rubble of vanished civilizations, and the only hope for ours.

Although this passage reflects a measured readability level which suggests that it would be easily within the grasp of most high school students (about ninth grade level), adolescents generally find it difficult to discuss. It is reasonable to suppose, in fact, that *some* adult remedial readers, despite their deficiencies in technical reading skills, *might* comprehend more in this case because of their broader living experiences.

The above passage does not represent the sort of material with which adult remedial readers typically experience conceptual difficulties. Adults who are learning to read are much more apt to be motivated toward materials which are of more immediate practical relevance to their lives and work. This selection merely illustrates that much printed material carries meaning that may render it incomprehensible to readers without background in the subject matter. The teacher needs to be alert to this potential problem so that he may attempt to cope with it when necessary. He may suggest that the student begin with simpler material in the same general subject area or help him acquire the necessary background through means other than reading. This may be undertaken through conversations and interviews with knowledgeable persons, films, and observations and practical experiences of various types. If the student wishes to read about a particular skill (how to operate a certain piece of equipment, for example), he is best served by observing and talking to someone else performing the skill in question. In this manner the student begins to acquire a conceptual framework which provides a foundation for further reading and refining his knowledge.

One further area of potential reading difficulties, related to conceptual framework, needs to be discussed. The reader may already have the necessary background to comprehend *if* he has some expectations as to what he is reading about. The adult remedial reader may frequently be so intent upon "getting the words right" that he is not properly attentive to, or loses track of, advance organizers which would help him predict meaning. Without advance organizers, even the skilled reader is frequently lost. Consider this passage (source unknown) and the questions which follow it:

The procedure is actually quite simple. First you arrange things into different groups. Of course one pile may be sufficient, depending on how much there is to do. If you have to go somewhere else due to lack of facilities, that is the next step; otherwise you are pretty well set. It is important not to overdo things. That is, it is better to do too few things at once than too many. In the short run, this may not seem important, but complications can easily arise. A mistake can be expensive as well. At first the whole procedure will seem complicated. Soon, however, it will become just another facet of life. It is difficult to foresee any end to the necessity for this task in the immediate future, but then one never can tell. After the procedure is completed one arranges the materials into different groups again. Then they can be put into their appropriate places. Eventually they will be used once more and the whole cycle will then have to be repeated. However, that is a part of life.

1.  What do you do to things first?
    a)   work simply
    b)   arrange them
    c)   put them into a single group
    d)   go elsewhere

2.  What happens if you have to go elsewhere?
    a)   you go on to the next step
    b)   you give up
    c)   you are set
    d)   you go elsewhere

3. What could be costly?
   a) an overload
   b) the procedure
   c) an error
   d) complications

4. When does this task cease to appear complex?
   a) when it becomes a habit
   b) in the beginning
   c) after many years
   d) when there is an end to the task

5. What is a part of life?
   a) the procedure
   b) the various facets
   c) the repetition
   d) the mistakes

Even after reading the passage *and* answering the questions which follow it, most readers have difficulty summarizing the content. On the other hand, if they are given the same passage, preceded by the title "Washing Clothes," their comprehension and ability to summarize is considerably improved.

The teacher needs to ascertain whether the adult remedial reader has an experiential background for the content area in which he is attempting to read. If the student lacks this background, the teacher must undertake to help him acquire it. If the learner demonstrates some familiarity with the subject matter, the teacher must be sure that he knows what he is reading about and that he is capable of using advance organizers effectively; otherwise, the student may become overly concerned with word accuracy, thereby (ironically) losing the context which would help him with word identification. When this happens he loses his frame of reference for meaning and has difficulty assimilating new information.

Adult remedial readers (and teachers as well) are often inclined to define reading (implicitly at least) as "word calling" or ability to decode. As a result, it often seems to be assumed that the student who can identify the words has all the prerequisites for reading success. As the preceding discussion of conceptual framework suggests, this is not the case. The reader must have, and be able to apply, some background for the content he is trying to comprehend.

## Sense of Purpose

Assuming that the reader is reading to acquire specific information and that he knows what information he is seeking, reading purpose takes care of itself. Often, however, we tend to read without specific purpose or without deciding in advance what information we wish to acquire. When we read for recreation this is no problem, but when our objective is to master a specific content, we may lose sight of the forest for the trees. Stauffer (1975) comments as follows on the importance of directing purpose in learning in general and in reading in particular:

> It is significant to note that a basic element in strategies for learning is an intention, a problem, a set, or a question. Similarly, it is the purpose of a reader that determines not only his rate of reading, but also the nature and depth of his achievement . . .
>
> In other words, the reading-thinking process must begin in the mind of the reader. He must raise the questions, or if he accepts the questions someone else raises, he must make the questions his own by speculating about likely answers. To the reader belong both the responsibility and the tyranny of "a right answer." [p. 88]

What instructional implications does this bit of philosophy offer for the adult remedial reader? He needs, first, to be encouraged to decide at what level to read a particular selection. Is he merely skimming a passage to pick out a few specific facts? Is he scanning to get some sense of comparisons or "hows" or "whys"? Or is he reading for every detail?

Inexperienced readers often lose sight of the fact that reading as an information-gathering process does not usually call for total detailed recall of all the material covered. Often, in fact, by focusing on details that he doesn't really need, the reader may lose the general concepts that are most important to him. The task of setting strategic purposes is, of course, closely related to using advance organizers effectively, as discussed in the preceding section.

Reading purpose may be no more complicated than a simple overview of a passage motivated by curiosity. On the other hand, if specific information is sought, the reader must be trained to formulate specific questions. The teacher may help this process initially by presenting the reader *in advance* with a group of questions with which to approach a particular passage. Sometimes it is possible to construct model sets of questions which may be used repetitively for different selections of the same basic type. In the case of newspapers, for example, a student might seek the following general information from any news story:

1. What or who is the article telling about?
2. What happened?
3. Where did it happen?
4. When did it happen?
5. How did it happen?
6. Why did it happen?

On the other hand, for want ads, more specific questions are appropriate, though the same questions may be applied to a whole series of ads:

1. What kind of job does the ad describe?
2. Is experience necessary?
3. How much is the pay?
4. Where is the job located?
5. Is there a telephone number to call?
6. Does the job require any set amount of education or training?
7. Do you have to own a car?

Questions such as those above, and also those designed for particular reading assignments (where the same questions cannot be used repetitively), are the first step in stimulating students to set their own purposes for reading. It is important to note, of course, that the passage may not address questions to which the reader seeks answers. The fact that some reading purposes are not immediately fulfilled does not detract from the value of prereading questions as an aid to comprehension. It is, in fact, typical of mature readers that they often read to see *whether or not* they can locate particular information they are seeking. By initially providing his students with questions relating to particular passages, the teacher not only stimulates them to read for purpose but "models" the types of questions they may later ask themselves.

## Organizational Mechanics

Related to the concept of advance organizers is the idea of organizational mechanics. Suppose, for example, the adult student wishes to read a manual pertaining to a particular skill, trade, interest, or hobby in which he has a personal investment. Does he know how to use the table of contents, the glossary, the index, or the appendixes? Does he understand the significance of topic headings (or headlines), boldface type, italics, etc.? Can he read and comprehend charts and other graphics, or do these intended aids to comprehension complicate it? In short, does he understand how the manual (or newspaper or other publication) is organized and can he locate the material relevant to his needs?

It is not the purpose of this section to provide lessons on how to teach each of these skills. Many reading textbooks offer guidelines for doing this for publications pertaining to different content areas, and teachers can improvise methods for helping adults cope with organizational mechanics in reading matter related to their particular interests. The point is that these skills cannot be taken for granted; it must not be assumed that students have them because often this is not the case. We suggest that teachers examine the competence of "content readers" in these areas by devising simple and informal criterion reference tests to find out whether students are familiar with the technical organizational aspects of the material they are reading. If these "tests" reveal the need for instruction, it may be rendered. On the other hand, if a student is competent in his grasp of organizational mechanics, he need not, and should not, be taught what he already knows.

## Vocabulary

Often the printed matter which is of interest to adult remedial readers contains difficult vocabulary which requires special assistance. Although the adult student may have a strong speaking vocabulary, he is not used to seeing in print many of the terms he may use regularly in speech. Frequently, because of his occupational experience, he. will retain job-related terms extremely well after he has been introduced to their appearance in print, but initial familiarity should not be taken for granted.

In advising teachers to be sure that adult students become acquainted with the specialized vocabulary which they may encounter, we do not suggest that the only way to accomplish this is to identify all potentially difficult words in advance. At this point in their growing independence, adult remedial readers have acquired a considerable variety of word-attack skills. It is thus advisable that the student first be given the opportunity to identify difficult and unfamiliar words on his own. Since he often has substantial background in the areas in which he is reading, he may do this quite successfully. If not, he may benefit more from assistance after he has attempted to decode independently.

It is a commonplace experience, of course, even for mature readers, to encounter words in print with which they are unfamiliar. The adult reme-dial reader should learn to accept this experience as a normal condition and not to expect to know immediately every word with which he comes in contact. Then, when he encounters vocabulary with which he is unfamiliar, he can be encouraged to follow the same procedures as those observed by more experienced readers. First, he must try to make what sense he can of the passage without identifying the word he doesn't know. This effort may either give him the word (or its meaning) from the context or suggest that the word is unnecessary to the central thought of the passage. If the word in question remains unknown and is judged essential to the meaning, the adult student seeks assistance from another individual or from a dictionary, in the same manner as the experienced reader.

In summary, it is important that teachers be aware of the problems that specialized, technical, or otherwise difficult vocabulary may cause, even for adult students who have achieved high degrees of reading independence. While teachers should encourage students to be as self-sufficient as possible in attacking unfamiliar words, they should be ready to provide assistance when needed.

## Writing Styles

Depending on the subject matter, many books and manuals tend to emphasize a predominant mode of expression. Some writing is heavy with comparisons and contrasts, with classifications of various types, or with cause and effect. If a particular manual, for example, is characterized by emphasis on one of these (or other) modes of expression, it is important that the student be sensitive to that style and able to comprehend it. Such considerations as the simple fact that some lists of items in context are simple enumerations, without regard for order, are important when such lists are compared to chronological sequences where order is essential to understanding.

No teacher, of course, can teach students all aspects of different writing styles, nor would such an effort be practical. Nonetheless, it would help them to have their attention drawn to salient characteristics of the printed matter upon which their learning is immediately focused.

## Conclusion

When the adult learner reaches the point at which he can attempt independent content reading with any degree of confidence, the hardest part of the battle is won. Yet there are still a number of potential obstacles which the student may encounter in his efforts to read particular subject matter on his own. Although there are obviously no certain solutions, this section has attempted to address some important considerations.

# Sustained Silent Reading

Sustained silent reading (SSR) has been initiated successfully in many public schools. Its objective, as the name implies, is to develop in each student both the ability and the habit of reading silently without interruption for as long a period as possible. The following excerpt from an article by McCracken (1971), which describes how SSR works for school children, outlines the fundamentals of this procedure, which can be used effectively for adults as well.

1.  *Each student must read silently.* The implication of this rule is that the teacher believes that each student can read silently so that no student dares pretend he cannot. The teacher may state an "or else" to convince the reluctant readers that reading is the lesser of two evils and to convince all students that the teacher is very serious about the business of silent reading.
2.  *The teacher reads*, and permits no interruption of his reading. He reads adult fare in which he can become engrossed. The teacher must set an example. Many students have never known an adult to read a book.

3.  *Each student selects a single book* (or magazine or newspaper). No book changing is permitted. There must be a wide range of materials available. No student, able or remedial, should be chided for reading an easy book. The teacher has books or magazines available for the student who says he has forgotten. For the student who is reluctant to choose, the teacher may select the book, require what is to be read, and give the student questions to answer for homework. The next day, he will have chosen his own book.

4.  *A timer is used.* An alarm clock or cooking timer is placed so that no one knows how much time has elapsed. A wall clock will not work; the reluctant readers become clock watchers. Nor can the teacher act as the timer; students will interrupt to ask if time is up. Start with five to ten minutes. When the timer rings, the teacher says "Good. You sustained your reading today for ten minutes (or whatever). Continue reading silently if you wish." Most of the class will choose to continue and they will maintain their attention for twenty to fifty minutes more. The teacher notes their sustaining power and sets the time forward the next day so that it almost reaches the sustained reading time of the first student who quit.

5.  *There are absolutely no reports or records of any kind.* Students do not even keep a list of books they read. Book discussions, writing, and record keeping flow naturally as sustained silent reading becomes a habit, but nothing is required initially or the reluctant readers do not participate.

6.  *Begin with whole classes or larger groups of students heterogeneously grouped.* Groups of ten or fewer sometimes can't get started because the students feel free to comment or to ask for help. Large groups, ninety to one hundred students, in an open area, with two or more teachers participating, have begun with no difficulty. [p. 521]

Some of the "rules" described above may, of course, be considerably relaxed for adults. It shouldn't be necessary, for example, to have "or else" admonitions or rigid prohibitions (which tend to be threatening to adult students) about changing reading matter during a session, though it should be explained to students that the rationale for sustained silent reading emphasizes sticking with one choice, at least for the duration of a reading period.

Several aspects of the SSR procedure need to be highlighted. It is especially important that the teacher read—that he model sustained silent reading for his students, some of whom have had little opportunity to observe anyone read for any period of time. It is also important that each student be given the opportunity to select reading matter that he wants to read and, preferably, that he can manage without undue strain. The idea is for the inexperienced reader to convince himself both that he *can* read fluently and that this can be an informative and *enjoyable* experience. Even more important than the student's growth in reading ability while under instruction is his future application of that ability, after he leaves the classroom. It is hoped that the sustained silent reading experience will help to assure that he continues to read as widely and extensively as possible.

Finally, it should be noted that the period for sustained silent reading is gradually increased, so that students acquire the endurance to extend their concentration over progressively longer periods of time. It is crucial that teachers, in initiating SSR, begin with only five- to ten-minute time intervals and increase them, at first, only several minutes at a time. Although it may seem to the teacher, who is accustomed to silent reading, that these time elements are unnecessarily brief, he should keep in mind the analogy of physical exercise. A person unaccustomed to jogging or swimming, for example, must take care not to overexercise when he begins the activity. However, if he continues on a regular basis, he will increase his sustaining power substantially.

Sustained silent reading is pleasurable and informative, as well as helpful to the reading abilities of those who engage in it. It combines learning to read and reading to learn—and reading to enjoy.

# Chapter 8

# Reading Diagnosis and Assessment

Our position on reading diagnosis and assessment for illiterates differs from that in most adult remedial programs. As a general rule, we feel that too much testing is done for no necessary or worthwhile purpose. Placement and evaluation of progress may usually be achieved just as quickly and accurately through informal means.

For placement purposes, we have found it helpful simply to ask the adult illiterate what he can read now and what he would like to learn to read, and then observe his efforts with materials in both of these categories. Frequently, this procedure provides all the information necessary for instructional decisions. If the teacher feels that more background is required, he may employ a variety of nonstandardized devices, including, for example, retelling (paraphrase of passages read) and informal uses of miscue analysis and the cloze procedure. As a final option, short of standardized testing, the teacher may resort to an "unobtrusive" screening device such as that designed by West (1978). All of these diagnostic procedures (and others) will be discussed in this chapter.

Beyond the fact that standardized tests are often unnecessary, they suffer from a number of additional liabilities when used as tools for analyzing the reading abilities or achievement of adult illiterates. The prospect of any standardized test, especially one which is norm referenced, is extremely threatening to persons who are undereducated and unaccustomed to testing in general. We have firsthand testimony from our students that many of their educationally deficient friends and co-workers will not enroll in Adult Basic Education programs primarily because of anxiety about entry testing. Furthermore, the standardized tests most widely used in adult remedial programs tend to measure a number of sub-skills which can be conveniently scored in grade-level terms but which are apt to be unrelated to the learner's specific reading needs and purposes. As a result, these tests often fail to reflect accurately either the learner's ability level or the progress he has made. The situation as regards standardized tests for adult illiterates is similar to that described by Bob Samples in *The Metaphoric Mind*:

The mulla Nasrudin was busily searching about on his hands and knees in the dirt in front of his house.

"What are you looking for, Mulla?" asked a friend.

"My buttons . . . my buttons . . . I've lost my buttons," the mulla answered with vexation.

"Where did you lose them, Mulla?"

"Back there . . . back there in my house," said Nasrudin, angrily pointing into his house.

"Well . . . why do you search here?" asked the puzzled friend.

Nasrudin answered, "Because the light is so much better!" [p. 57]

As a society, Samples reflects further, we often tend to look for answers and to write rules merely on the basis of where there is "more light." Similarly, we tend to test in a manner that renders scoring which is precise but may be misrepresentative in terms of what it measures. Certainly in the adult student's case, the issue is not his grade level, or even how he compares with other students on particular reading subskills, but how he can be helped to read what he wants and needs in his daily life and work.

To develop our ideas relating to diagnosis and assessment, the remainder of our discussion will be divided into several major sections. First, we will focus in greater detail upon prevailing practices pertaining to assessment of the reading abilities of functional illiterates in Adult Basic Education programs, giving particular attention to our reservations about these practices. We will then discuss the reading needs of adult illiterates and their impact upon how reading abilities should be evaluated.

Our next section relates to various procedures which we have found helpful in making informal and nonquantitative assessments of reader behavior and to some important aspects of reading behavior which formal tests fail to measure.

Finally, we offer some thoughts on what sorts of quantitative devices might be employed for adult illiterates when teachers and/or administrators feel it necessary to use such instruments despite our reservations.

## Typical Evaluation Procedures

The prevailing practice in most public school adult reading and Adult Basic Education programs is to give students a test or series of tests at the time of their enrollment. Tests used for this purpose may be the same as those employed generally in public schools, the Gates-MacGinite, for example. In some instances these tests are designed for adults — such as the ABLE (Adult Basic Learning Examination) — and include subtests in reading and in other areas as well. Typically, reading subtests of these instruments provide grade-level measures on such reading "components" as speed, vocabulary, and comprehension. Often the same tests are used at the end of the academic year (or other logical break point) and pre- and post-test scores are compared to determine each student's change in grade level. These scores are also used, in some cases, by administrators to evaluate teachers and may be required by state departments of education as a prerequisite for continued program funding.

The fairly standard procedures described above create a number of difficulties, including demoralization of students and serious misconceptions about what represents progress for the adult remedial reader. These two issues are closely related and must be discussed together.

Frequently, it takes tremendous fortitude for the functionally illiterate adult to bring himself before the educational "establishment" with a declaration of vulnerability which amounts to "I can't read; teach me." Usually, the establishment responds by requiring the self-confessed illiterate to take a test in order to prove he can't (or at what level he can't) read. This can be a devastating experience for the extremely self-conscious adult remedial reader.

The problems created by forcing tests on adult remedial readers are exacerbated by the fact that such tests are usually norm referenced and contain many items which are *designed* to be too difficult for most testees. The purpose of norm-referenced tests is to compare the abilities of students, usually in terms of grade levels, and this can be accomplished only with a variety of items that reflect a broad range of difficulty. Criterion-referenced tests, which *describe* rather than *compare* student performance, often make more sense in Adult Basic Education and remedial reading programs where the emphasis is upon equipping a student with the literacy skills he needs in his life rather than upon raising his relative grade-level standing. Even in the case of criterion-referenced tests, however, there are potential difficulties. Adult learners differ not only in their criteria for success, depending upon their individual interests and needs, but in their reading goals themselves.

Whatever the nature of the entry test for adult illiterates, these students are apt to be totally unfamiliar with the testing situation and to feel threatened by it. Such circumstances not only result in questionable measures of learner abilities but are also a severe detriment to student morale. Where adults must repeat testing at the end of their programs, they are often demoralized again. Whether or not they are given access to their standardized test scores, remedial readers are often aware that their scores show no improvement. It some cases, test scores may even decline. This does not necessarily mean, however, that no reading growth has occurred. What must be carefully considered are the aims of the program and the objectives of particular adult students.

Most adult remedial readers are interested in learning to read in contexts related to their occupations and other mainstream life activities. Perceptive teachers thus focus their instruction accordingly, paying little attention to the reading of testlike material. In such cases a student's test scores may fail to show significant improvement, since he was not only unfamiliar with tests to begin with but has not had instruction and practice focusing on testlike items. On the other hand, his reading independence may have grown substantially in terms of his learning objectives and his ability to cope with the real-life reading matter that has previously handicapped him.

It should be noted at this point that it is usually possible to raise test scores when teacher and student decide that this should be a top priority. The author worked at one time in a literacy training unit in the navy that was more than 90 percent successful in converting test "failures" to "passers" in a four-week period. Test-score improvement was in this instance the top priority of the instructional program, since the navy recruits involved needed to improve their scores to avoid "flunking out" of the navy. As a result, a great deal of time was devoted to testlike exercises and very little to the literacy needs of the sailors themselves beyond this narrow context.

## The Reading Needs of the Functional Illiterate

In the final analysis, literacy is a personal matter. In real-life terms, the individual is neither labeled as nor caused to feel illiterate until he fails to cope with the literacy requirements of his work or other life roles. Progress in these areas can thus be justly regarded as literacy development.

The functional illiterate's reading needs are always situation specific, and his progress can be meaningfully measured only in terms of the relative levels of independence he achieves in working toward his goals. Although some increase in test performance often accompanies growth in independence related to particular occupation- and life-oriented reading tasks, this is by no means always true. In any case, the perceptive teacher focuses instruction on individual needs and interests. Learning tasks are directed toward real-life materials, not test-like exercises, unless the latter are related to a particular learner objective (for example, passing a written test for a driver's license).

The situation can be illustrated by the progress of a student who wanted to read the daily newspaper. In the beginning, the mere thought of undertaking this task was overwhelming. Because he could make no sense of first-page stories, the student was on the verge of concluding that his goal was beyond him. He had only a vague idea of other types of newspaper reading matter and no sense of where different types of content might be located in the paper. Although this student was a struggling reader, he eventually (over a period of months in a two-night-a-week program) achieved a remarkable degree of independence with a newspaper. He could locate and comprehend the answers to specific questions relating to such items as weather forecasts, the movie page, sports stories, and the classified ads. Finally, he acquired sufficient confidence to read a news story on his own initiative. He could not read every word but could comprehend enough to acquire and retain as much information as most mature readers.

This evolution of independence occurred over an entire academic year, while the student was involved in a variety of other personally selected reading and writing tasks as well. At the end of the year, however, his ABLE reading scores were about the same as they had been at the beginning. This was not altogether surprising. At no point was his reading instruction focused on testlike items, and the process of testing had been a totally unfamiliar situation.

The crux of the matter is that adult reading needs are always life related. Perceptive teachers realize this and focus their instruction accordingly. Most standardized tests, on the other hand, are norm based and reflect improvement only in terms of grade levels, not in terms of reading independence and specific individual goals.

## What Tests Fail to Measure

Even if standardized tests could be accepted as providing valid and adequate measures of adult reading gains, there would still be a danger of attaching too much significance to test scores. Much of the worth of an educational program cannot be measured in any standardized manner. In the case of the adult reading programs, tests do not tell us, for example, what attitudes toward reading are fostered in students or what students' continued application of reading will be. These elements, which are probably the most crucial in terms of overall learning impact, are not measured at all. In his adult-education text, Houle (1972) warns against the danger of allowing precise measures of program components (which *can* be measured) to represent total program evaluation. This caution is particularly appropriate for reading programs. There has often been a tendency by students, teachers, and administrators to make sweeping judgments, based on a few test scores, which may not even address primary learning interests and needs.

# Informal Assessments (Nonquantitative)

Teachers are often inclined (and influenced) to discount their observations of a remedial reader's progress in favor of a group of test scores. Although use of a particular test is often justified on a number of grounds (it is "better" than other tests; it comes accompanied by an impressive "track record," supported by pages of data; or it has "always been used"), the fact is that a teacher's observations of an adult student's progress and the student's self-evaluations are often the most meaningful assessments that can be made. It remains true, of course, that the teacher of adult remedial reading often needs assistance in determining an appropriate frame of reference in which to evaluate student success.

In making informal assessments of adult reading abilities, several important generalizations should be kept in mind. Evaluation should be qualitative rather than quantitative. The primary emphasis should be on the reader's ability to comprehend meaning from print, as opposed to his ability to pronounce words represented by printed symbols. It follows that, where possible, evaluation should focus on silent rather than oral reading performance. The student, as well as the teacher, needs to be thoroughly acquainted with these generalizations and the rationale which underlies them.

Rather than focusing simply on the quantity of technical miscues or reading "mistakes," as is the case with quantitative measures, qualitative assessment is concerned with the nature of these so-called errors. At the beginning stage of assessment the student is asked to read orally in order to give the teacher maximum information about how he approaches the printed page. Since the emphasis is on fluency, however, rather than on precise accuracy in pronouncing word-symbol correspondences, interruptions are kept to a minimum. The student is told that he will not be immediately corrected if he skips or mispronounces a word. He is encouraged, in fact, "to read beyond" unfamiliar words for context and to supply them later if he is able. If the student thinks he knows a particular word, he is encouraged to try it and keep going, correcting himself if eventually he decides his original choice does not make sense. When he has finished reading, he may be asked to retell, in his own words, what he has read.

In reviewing the reader's "performance" (usually on tape, to avoid note-taking, which may be diverting, the teacher asks himself a number of questions, based on the reader's miscues or on "wrong" words instead of "right" words. Sample questions might be:

1.  Does the substitution make sense in the context?
2.  Is the substitution's part of speech the same (or does it fit as appropriately in context) as that of the "correct" word?
3.  How closely does the spelling of the substituted word resemble that of the correct word?
4.  Does the dialect of the speaker have a significant impact on the miscue?

The rationale for questions of this type is set forth in Burke and Goodman's *Reading Miscue Inventory* (1972). We do not recommend that the teacher employ the RMI itself with most adult readers; the full inventory is extremely intricate, time consuming, and difficult to score. The rationale on which it is based, however, is valuable background for any reading teacher, perhaps especially for the teacher of adult students because of the adult's longer and more complicated background with language.

The fact that the purpose of qualitative assessment is to understand how the remedial reader thinks, rather than simply to judge his technical proficiency, is significant for the adult student in other respects. Since adult remedial readers have a history of failure in circumstances where others have learned to read, it is important to acquire maximum insight into *why* they have not been successful. To the extent that the teacher's qualitative assessment can tie into the reader's thought process, he can begin to accentuate the positive aspects of the learner's efforts to make sense of print. Further, he can help the learner become his own diagnostician by helping him ask himself such questions as:

1.  Does this sound like language to me?
2.  Does this make sense to me?

Fluent readers implicitly ask themselves these questions on a continuous basis as they process print. Beginning readers, however, can easily become preoccupied with decoding individual words and lose overall meaning. The informal assessment process thus assumes a teaching as well as a diagnostic function, and the adult remedial reader can approach his task with more confidence and a greater opportunity to achieve fluency

The second generalization, that informal assessment should emphasize comprehension of meaning rather than precise accuracy in pronunciation of words, follows from the implications of the first. Reading is a process not of parroting words but of making sense of print. The adult reader has successfully read a job order when he is able to understand the message intended by the writer. He has read the newspaper when (for example) he is able to comprehend from newsprint what conditions the weather bureau is predicting. This is true whether or not he can decode every word.

The third generalization, pertaining to silent and oral reading, follows automatically from the second. Silent reading always emphasizes meaning, as opposed to precision. Also, silent reading in the classroom much more closely approximates the real-life conditions confronted by adult readers. The only constructive purpose of oral reading for beginning readers is to allow the teacher to form some sense of how proficiently the learner can decode print and, qualitatively, what sort of reading miscues he makes. Once the teacher acquires this information, the emphasis of instruction and assessment should be on silent reading.

# Evaluating Comprehension

Once the teacher has completed a qualitative assessment of the learner's thinking as he approaches reading, he may ask the student to retell what he has read as an indication of his comprehension. Here again, caution is in order. The reader is somewhat under fire, since he knows he was being diagnosed as he read. Before attaching too much significance to this initial retelling, the teacher should give the student the opportunity to retell some material he has read silently under less trying conditions. If necessary, the teacher may stimulate retelling by asking leading questions.

In addition to retelling, comprehension in silent reading can be checked in several other ways. The reader can be given questions, either before he has read, in order to see if he can direct his reading purposes, or after he has read. Another good comprehension check is the cloze procedure, in which the student is presented with a passage in which every fifth word (for example) has been deleted and he is asked to fill in the missing words. "Official" cloze scoring directions usually require that the student supply the exact word which was deleted for purposes of standardizing scoring procedures. When the cloze procedure is used informally, however, the teacher is under no such constraint. His purpose is simply to observe the extent to which the student can fill in either the words which were deleted or alternatives which are both syntactically and semantically appropriate in the context.

# When Testing Is Inevitable

We have stated a number of concerns about formal testing of adult remedial readers; nonetheless, there are times when funding stipulations and other program requirements dictate that some means of formal testing be employed for both screening and placement purposes and as a measure of learning (and instructional) effectiveness. Where teachers have a choice of instruments to employ, there are some necessary considerations to be kept in mind.

A possible means of reducing student anxiety about entry testing (short of the ideal of not testing at all) is an "unobtrusive screening device" such as that designed by West (1978). The WIRE (West Informal Reading Inventory), as this instrument is called, has two alternative forms. Each consists of three questions pertaining to adult education classes (how students travel to class, how teachers could make classes better, etc.), which students read and respond to in writing. Since these questions are expressed in vocabulary and syntax which become progressively more difficult, the teacher can draw inferences as to the learner's reading ability from the number of questions to which he is able to respond meaningfully. The three questions of each form of WIRE reflect reading abilities at the third, sixth, and ninth grade levels.

The designer of WIRE has presented evidence that its results on both versions correlate with those of the RFU (Reading for Understanding) diagnostic instrument at higher than .8, and it may well be that WIRE correlates highly with the results achieved through much more complicated instruments for measuring reading comprehension. Nonetheless, while WIRE or similar devices may be very effective in some instances, it is doubtful that they are always a successful means of counteracting anxiety in beginning students. If an individual realizes that he is incapable of filling out a precourse questionnaire, it cannot encourage him in regard to his learning prospects under actual instruction. Also, in the case of an instrument such as WIRE, which requires that respondents both read and write, it may be difficult to determine whether student deficiencies lie in one or both of these areas.

In regard to more conventional tests and evaluation instruments, it is not our purpose to analyze any instrument in detail. Tests for adult functional illiterates are widely discussed in a number of other sources, including Bowren and Zintz (1977) and Nafziger, Thompson, Hiscox, and Owen (1976). The latter, in their *Tests of Functional Adult Literacy: An Evaluation of Currently Available Instruments*, present an analysis of all tests they could locate pertaining to functional literacy (see table 7). The book contains detailed discussions—including publisher, description, availability of alternate forms, administration time, procedures, materials, and scoring procedures—for seventeen tests. Four tests are criterion referenced, five are norm referenced, and eight are labeled "informal" (though they are much more formal and systematic than the evaluation procedures we recommended earlier). In addition, the authors present a detailed rating chart which compares and evaluates more than thirty tests in various aspects of four general criteria: measurement validity, examinee appropriateness (factors having to do primarily with format and comprehensibility), technical evidence (mainly reliability) and administrative usability. Each test is then rated "poor," "fair," or "good" in each of the four areas.

TABLE 7. TESTS FOR THE ADULT FUNCTIONAL ILLITERATES

| TEST NAME | MEASUREMENT VALIDITY | | EXAMINEE APPROPRIATENESS | | | | | | | | | | | |
|---|---|---|---|---|---|---|---|---|---|---|---|---|---|
| | | | | | Compre-hension | | Format | | | | | | |
| | Content and Construct | Concurrent and Predictive | Justification | Item Relevance | Content | Instructions | Layout | Illustration/ Print Quality | Auditory Presentation | Coherence | Response Mode | Recording Responses | Power Test |
| Rating Range ➡ | 0-8 | 0-4 | 0-1 | 0-1 | 0-2 | 0-4 | 0-1 | 0-1 | 0-1 | 0-1 | | 0-2 | 0-1 |
| I. CRITERION-REFERENCED FUNCTIONAL LITERACY TESTS | | | | | | | | | | | | | |
| ADULT PERFORMANCE LEVEL | 7 | 0 | 1 | 1 | 2 | 3 | 1 | 1 | 1 | 1 | Mi | 2 | 1 |
| BASIC SKILLS READING MASTERY TEST | 7 | 0 | 0 | 1 | 2 | 3 | 1 | 1 | 1 | 1 | Wr | 1 | 1 |
| READING/EVERYDAY ACTIVITIES IN LIFE | 7 | 2 | 1 | 1 | 2 | 4 | 1 | 1 | 1 | 1 | Wr | 2 | 1 |
| WISCONSIN TEST OF ADULT BASIC ED., Life Coping Skills | 6 | 0 | 0 | 1 | 2 | 2 | 1 | 1 | 0 | 1 | Wr | 2 | 1 |
| | | | | | | | | | | | | | |
| II. STANDARDIZED TESTS | | | | | | | | | | | | | |
| A. General Educational Development Performance Tests | | | | | | | | | | | | | |
| GEN. EDUCATIONAL PERFORMANCE INDEX, Correctness & Effectiveness of Expression | 5 | 1 | 1 | 1 | 1 | 3 | 1 | 1 | 0 | 1 | Wr | 1 | 1 |
| GEN. EDUCATIONAL PERFORMANCE INDEX, Literary Interpretation | 5 | 1 | 1 | 0 | 1 | 2 | 1 | 1 | 0 | 1 | Wr | 1 | 1 |
| | | | | | | | | | | | | | |
| B. Multiple Reading Skills Tests | | | | | | | | | | | | | |
| SRA READING INDEX | 6 | 1 | 0 | 1 | 1 | 4 | 1 | 1 | 1 | 1 | Wr | 2 | 1 |
| WISCONSIN TEST OF ADULT BASIC ED., Word Meaning and Reading | 6 | 0 | 0 | 0 | 1 | 2 | 1 | 1 | 0 | 1 | Wr | 2 | 1 |
| | | | | | | | | | | | | | |
| | | | | | | | | | | | | | |
| | | | | | | | | | | | | | |

Note:    The body of the table includes the ratings assigned to each test for individual criteria. A figure of zero on any criterion indicates noncompliance or lack of information.

The meanings of the symbols under "Response Mode" are as follows: "Or" — Oral; "Wr" — Written; and "Mi" — Mixed.

Reprinted by permission, from Tests of Functional Adult Literacy: An Evaluation of Currently Available Instruments, by Dean Nafziger, R. Brent Thompson, Michael D. Hiscox, and Thomas R. Owen (Portland: Northwest Regional Educational Laboratory, 1977).

Table 7. (Continued)

| TECHNICAL EXCELLENCE | | | | ADMINISTRATIVE USABILITY | | | | | | | | | | | | | | | | TOTAL GRADES |
|---|---|---|---|---|---|---|---|---|---|---|---|---|---|---|---|---|---|---|---|---|
| Reliability | | | | Administration | | | | | Interpretation | | | | | | | | | | | |
| Alternate Form | Test-Retest | Internal Consistency | Replicability | Training of Admin. | Admin. Time | Clarity of Manual | Number of Admin. | Scoring | Training | Range | Diversity | Score Conversion | Interpre. | Real Life Skills | Validating Group | Racial/Ethnic/Sex Represent. | Can Decisions Be Made? | Alternate Forms | Form Comparability | |
| 0-3 | 0-3 | 0-2 | 0-1 | 0-1 | 0-1 | 0-1 | 0-1 | 0-2 | 0-1 | 0-1 | 0-1 | 0-2 | 0-1 | 0-1 | 0-1 | 0-2 | 0-2 | 0-1 | 0-1 | Good-Fair-Poor |
| | | | | | | | | | | | | | | | | | | | | |
| 0 | 0 | 0 | 1 | 1 | 0 | 1 | 1 | 1 | 1 | 1 | 1 | 0 | 0 | 1 | 1 | 2 | 0 | 0 | 0 | FGPP |
| 0 | 0 | 2 | 1 | 1 | 0 | 1 | 1 | 2 | 1 | 1 | 1 | 2 | 1 | 1 | 0 | 0 | 0 | 0 | 0 | FGFF |
| 0 | 0 | 2 | 1 | 1 | 0 | 1 | 1 | 1 | 1 | 1 | 1 | 2 | 1 | 1 | 0 | 2 | 2 | 0 | 0 | FGFF |
| 0 | 0 | 2 | 1 | 1 | 0 | 0 | 1 | 1 | 1 | 1 | 1 | 0 | 0 | 0 | 0 | 1 | 0 | 0 | 0 | FFFP |
| | | | | | | | | | | | | | | | | | | | | |
| | | | | | | | | | | | | | | | | | | | | |
| 1 | 0 | 0 | 1 | 1 | 0 | 1 | 1 | 2 | 1 | 0 | 1 | 1 | 1 | 0 | 1 | 2 | 1 | 1 | 1 | FFPF |
| 0 | 0 | 0 | 1 | 1 | 0 | 1 | 1 | 2 | 1 | 0 | 1 | 1 | 1 | 0 | 1 | 2 | 1 | 1 | 1 | FFPF |
| | | | | | | | | | | | | | | | | | | | | |
| 0 | 0 | 1 | 1 | 1 | 0 | 1 | 1 | 2 | 1 | 1 | 1 | 2 | 1 | 0 | 0 | 2 | 2 | 0 | 0 | FGPF |
| 0 | 0 | 2 | 1 | 1 | 1 | 0 | 1 | 2 | 1 | 1 | 1 | 0 | 0 | 0 | 0 | 1 | 0 | 0 | 0 | FFFP |
| | | | | | | | | | | | | | | | | | | | | |
| | | | | | | | | | | | | | | | | | | | | |
| | | | | | | | | | | | | | | | | | | | | |

The entries under Total Grades summarize test performance on the four major criterion areas, in this order:  1. Measurement Validity, 2. Examinee Appropriateness, 3. Technical Excellence, and 4. Administrative Usability.  Thus, the entry "PGFF" is to be interpreted:
  Poor for Measurement Validity
  Good for Examinee Appropriateness
  Fair for Technical Excellence
  Fair for Administrative Usability

TABLE 7. (Continued)

| TEST NAME | MEASUREMENT VALIDITY | | Justification | Item Relevance | Comprehension | | Format | | | | Response Mode | Recording Responses | Power Test |
|---|---|---|---|---|---|---|---|---|---|---|---|---|---|
| | Content and Construct | Concurrent and Predictive | | | Content | Instructions | Layout | Illustration/ Print Quality | Auditory Presentation | Coherence | | | |
| Rating Range ➡ | 0-8 | 0-4 | 0-1 | 0-1 | 0-2 | 0-4 | 0-1 | 0-1 | 0-1 | 0-1 | | 0-2 | 0-1 |
| C. Reading Comprehension Tests | | | | | | | | | | | | | |
| ADULT BASIC LEARNING EXAMINATION, Reading | 5 | 1 | 1 | 1 | 1 | 4 | 1 | 1 | 1 | 1 | Wr | 2 | 1 |
| BASIC OCCUPATIONAL LITERACY TEST, Comprehension | 4 | 0 | 1 | 1 | 1 | 4 | 1 | 1 | 1 | 1 | Wr | 2 | 1 |
| TESTS OF ADULT BASIC EDUCATION, Comprehension | 4 | 0 | 1 | 1 | 1 | 4 | 1 | 1 | 1 | 1 | Wr | 1 | 0 |
| | | | | | | | | | | | | | |
| D. Spelling Tests | | | | | | | | | | | | | |
| ADULT BASIC LEARNING EXAMINATION, Spelling | 6 | 2 | 1 | 1 | 2 | 3 | 1 | 1 | 1 | 1 | Wr | 2 | 1 |
| | | | | | | | | | | | | | |
| E. Vocabulary Tests | | | | | | | | | | | | | |
| ADULT BASIC LEARNING EXAMINATION, Vocabulary | 5 | 1 | 1 | 1 | 2 | 4 | 1 | 1 | 1 | 1 | Wr | 2 | 1 |
| BASIC OCCUPATIONAL LITERACY TEST, Vocabulary | 4 | 0 | 1 | 1 | 1 | 4 | 1 | 1 | 1 | 1 | Wr | 2 | 1 |
| TESTS OF ADULT BASIC EDUCATION, Vocabulary | 4 | 0 | 1 | 1 | 1 | 4 | 1 | 1 | 1 | 1 | Wr | 1 | 0 |
| | | | | | | | | | | | | | |
| | | | | | | | | | | | | | |
| | | | | | | | | | | | | | |
| | | | | | | | | | | | | | |
| | | | | | | | | | | | | | |

Note:    The body of the table includes the ratings assigned to each test for individual criteria.
         A figure of zero on any criterion indicates noncompliance or lack of information.

         The meanings of the symbols under "Response Mode" are as follows:
         "Or" — Oral; "Wr" — Written; and "Mi" — Mixed.

TABLE 7. (Continued)

| TECHNICAL EXCELLENCE | | | | ADMINISTRATIVE USABILITY | | | | | | | | | | | | | | | | |
| Reliability | | | | Administration | | | | | Interpretation | | | | | | | | | | | TOTAL GRADES |
| Alternate Form | Test-Retest | Internal Consistency | Replicability | Training of Admin. | Admin. Time | Clarity of Manual | Number of Admin. | Scoring | Training | Range | Diversity | Score Conversion | Interpre. | Real Life Skills | Validating Group | Racial/Ethnic/Sex Represent. | Can Decisions Be Made? | Alternate Forms | Form Comparability | |
| 0-3 | 0-3 | 0-2 | 0-1 | 0-1 | 0-1 | 0-1 | 0-1 | 0-2 | 0-1 | 0-1 | 0-1 | 0-2 | 0-1 | 0-1 | 0-1 | 0-2 | 0-2 | 0-1 | 0-1 | Good-Fair-Poor |
| | | | | | | | | | | | | | | | | | | | | |
| 0 | 0 | 2 | 1 | 1 | 0 | 1 | 1 | 2 | 1 | 1 | 1 | 2 | 1 | 0 | 0 | 2 | 1 | 1 | 1 | FGFG |
| 0 | 0 | 0 | 1 | 1 | 1 | 1 | 1 | 2 | 1 | 0 | 1 | 2 | 0 | 0 | 0 | 2 | 2 | 1 | 1 | PGPG |
| 0 | 0 | 0 | 0 | 1 | 0 | 1 | 1 | 2 | 1 | 1 | 1 | 2 | 1 | 0 | 0 | 0 | 2 | 1 | 1 | PGPF |
| | | | | | | | | | | | | | | | | | | | | |
| | | | | | | | | | | | | | | | | | | | | |
| 0 | 0 | 2 | 1 | 1 | 1 | 1 | 1 | 2 | 1 | 1 | 1 | 2 | 1 | 0 | 0 | 2 | 1 | 1 | 1 | FGFG |
| | | | | | | | | | | | | | | | | | | | | |
| | | | | | | | | | | | | | | | | | | | | |
| 0 | 0 | 1 | 1 | 1 | 1 | 1 | 1 | 2 | 1 | 1 | 1 | 2 | 1 | 0 | 0 | 2 | 2 | 1 | 1 | FGPG |
| 0 | 0 | 0 | 1 | 1 | 1 | 1 | 1 | 2 | 1 | 0 | 1 | 2 | 0 | 0 | 0 | 2 | 2 | 1 | 1 | PGPG |
| 0 | 0 | 0 | 0 | 1 | 1 | 1 | 1 | 2 | 1 | 1 | 1 | 2 | 1 | 0 | 0 | 0 | 2 | 1 | 1 | PGPG |
| | | | | | | | | | | | | | | | | | | | | |
| | | | | | | | | | | | | | | | | | | | | |
| | | | | | | | | | | | | | | | | | | | | |
| | | | | | | | | | | | | | | | | | | | | |
| | | | | | | | | | | | | | | | | | | | | |
| | | | | | | | | | | | | | | | | | | | | |

The entries under Total Grades summarize test performance on the four major criterion areas, in this order: 1. Measurement Validity, 2. Examinee Appropriateness, 3. Technical Excellence, and 4. Administrative Usability. Thus, the entry "PGFF" is to be interpreted:

> Poor for Measurement Validity
> Good for Examinee Appropriateness
> Fair for Technical Excellence
> Fair for Adminstrative Usability

TABLE 7.  (Continued)

| TEST NAME | MEASUREMENT VALIDITY | | EXAMINEE APPROPRIATENESS | | | | | | | | | | | |
| | Content and Construct | Concurrent and Predictive | Justification | Item Relevance | Content (Compre-hension) | Instructions (Compre-hension) | Layout | Illustration/Print Quality | Auditory Presentation | Coherence | Response Mode | Recording Responses | Power Test |
| Rating Range ➡ | 0-8 | 0-4 | 0-1 | 0-1 | 0-2 | 0-4 | 0-1 | 0-1 | 0-1 | 0-1 | | 0-2 | 0-1 |
| III.  INFORMAL TESTS | | | | | | | | | | | | | |
| A.  Oral Reading Tests | | | | | | | | | | | | | |
| INFORMAL TEXTBOOK TEST | 1 | 0 | 0 | 1 | 1 | 1 | 1 | 0 | 0 | 1 | Wr | 2 | 1 |
| IDAHO STATE PENITENTIARY INFORMAL READING INVENTORY | 3 | 0 | 0 | 1 | 2 | 3 | 1 | 1 | 0 | 1 | Or | 2 | 1 |
| IND. READING PLACEMENT INVENTORY, Oral Paragraph Reading | 4 | 2 | 0 | 1 | 1 | 1 | 1 | 1 | 0 | 1 | Or | 2 | 1 |
| IND. READING PLACEMENT INVENTORY, Present Language Potential | 4 | 2 | 0 | 1 | 1 | 1 | 1 | 1 | 0 | 1 | Or | 2 | 1 |
| INFORMAL READING INVENTORY, Oral Reading | 0 | 0 | 0 | 1 | 1 | 1 | 0 | 0 | 0 | 1 | Or | 2 | 1 |
| INFORMAL READING INVENTORY, Present Potential Level | 0 | 0 | 0 | 1 | 1 | 1 | 1 | 0 | 0 | 1 | Or | 2 | 1 |
| INITIAL TESTING LOCATOR TESTS | 0 | 0 | 0 | 1 | 1 | 0 | 1 | 0 | 0 | 1 | Mi | 2 | 1 |
| READING EVALUATION - ADULT DIAGNOSIS Reading Inventory | 1 | 0 | 1 | 1 | 1 | 3 | 1 | 1 | 1 | 1 | Or | 2 | 1 |
| | | | | | | | | | | | | | |
| B. Reading Comprehension Tests | | | | | | | | | | | | | |
| ADULT BASIC READING INVENTORY, Context Reading | 0 | 2 | 1 | 1 | 1 | 3 | 1 | 1 | 1 | 1 | Wr | 2 | 1 |
| | | | | | | | | | | | | | |
| C.  Recognition or Discrimination Tests | | | | | | | | | | | | | |
| ADULT BASIC READING INVENTORY, Sight words | 0 | 0 | 1 | 1 | 1 | 4 | 1 | 1 | 1 | 1 | Wr | 2 | 1 |
| ADULT BASIC READING INVENTORY, Sound and Letter Discrimination | 0 | 0 | 1 | 1 | 1 | 4 | 1 | 1 | 1 | 1 | Wr | 2 | 1 |

Note:    The body of the table includes the ratings assigned to each test for individual criteria.
A figure of zero on any criterion indicates noncompliance or lack of information.

The meanings of the symbols under "Response Mode" are as follows:
"Or" — Oral;  "Wr" — Written;  and "Mi" — Mixed.

TABLE 7. (Continued)

| Alternate Form | Test-Retest | Internal Consistency | Replicability | Training of Admin. | Admin. Time | Clarity of Manual | Number of Admin. | Scoring | Training | Range | Diversity | Score Conversion | Interpre. | Real Life Skills | Validating Group | Racial/Ethnic/Sex Represent. | Can Decisions Be Made? | Alternate Forms | Form Comparability | TOTAL GRADES |
|---|---|---|---|---|---|---|---|---|---|---|---|---|---|---|---|---|---|---|---|---|
| 0-3 | 0-3 | 0-2 | 0-1 | 0-1 | 0-1 | 0-1 | 0-1 | 0-2 | 0-1 | 0-1 | 0-1 | 0-2 | 0-1 | 0-1 | 0-1 | 0-2 | 0-2 | 0-1 | 0-1 | Good-Fair-Poor |
|  |  |  |  |  |  |  |  |  |  |  |  |  |  |  |  |  |  |  |  |  |
|  |  |  |  |  |  |  |  |  |  |  |  |  |  |  |  |  |  |  |  |  |
| 0 | 0 | 0 | 0 | 1 | 1 | 0 | 1 | 1 | 1 | 1 | 0 | 2 | 1 | 0 | 0 | 0 | 1 | 0 | 0 | PFPP |
| 0 | 0 | 0 | 0 | 1 | 0 | 1 | 1 | 1 | 1 | 1 | 0 | 1 | 1 | 0 | 0 | 0 | 2 | 1 | 1 | PGPF |
| 3 | 0 | 0 | 1 | 1 | 1 | 1 | 1 | 1 | 1 | 1 | 1 | 2 | 1 | 0 | 0 | 0 | 2 | 1 | 1 | FFFF |
| 3 | 0 | 0 | 1 | 1 | 1 | 1 | 1 | 1 | 1 | 1 | 1 | 2 | 1 | 0 | 0 | 0 | 2 | 1 | 1 | FFFF |
| 0 | 0 | 0 | 0 | 1 | 0 | 0 | 1 | 1 | 1 | 1 | 1 | 0 | 1 | 0 | 0 | 0 | 1 | 0 | 0 | PPPP |
| 0 | 0 | 0 | 0 | 1 | 0 | 0 | 1 | 1 | 1 | 1 | 1 | 2 | 1 | 0 | 0 | 0 | 1 | 0 | 0 | PFPP |
| 0 | 0 | 0 | 0 | 1 | 1 | 0· | 1 | 1 | 1 | 1 | 0 | 0 | 1 | 0 | 0 | 0 | 1 | 0 | 0 | PPPP |
| 0 | 0 | 0 | 0 | 1 | 0 | 0 | 1 | 1 | 1 | 1 | 1 | 2 | 1 | 0 | 0 | 0 | 1 | 1 | 1 | PGPF |
|  |  |  |  |  |  |  |  |  |  |  |  |  |  |  |  |  |  |  |  |  |
|  |  |  |  |  |  |  |  |  |  |  |  |  |  |  |  |  |  |  |  |  |
| 0 | 0 | 2 | 1 | 1 | 1 | 0 | 1 | 2 | 1 | 1 | 1 | 2 | 1 | 0 | 0 | 0 | 2 | 0 | 0 | PGFF |
|  |  |  |  |  |  |  |  |  |  |  |  |  |  |  |  |  |  |  |  |  |
|  |  |  |  |  |  |  |  |  |  |  |  |  |  |  |  |  |  |  |  |  |
| 0 | 0 | 2 | 1 | 1 | 1 | 0 | 1 | 2 | 1 | 0 | 1 | 2 | 1 | 0 | 0 | 0 | 0 | 0 | 0 | PGFP |
| 0 | 0 | 2 | 1 | 1 | 1 | 0 | 1 | 2 | 1 | 0 | 1 | 2 | 0 | 0 | 0 | 0 | 1 | 0 | 0 | PGFP |

The entries under Total Grades summarize test performance on the four major criterion areas, in this order, 1. Measurement Validity, 2. Examinee Appropriateness, 3. Technical Excellence, and 4. Administrative Usability. Thus, the entry "PGFF" is to be interpreted:
> Poor for Measurement Validity
> Good for Examinee Appropriateness
> Fair for Technical Excellence
> Fair for Administrative Usability

TABLE 7.  (Continued)

| TEST NAME | MEASUREMENT VALIDITY | | | EXAMINEE APPROPRIATENESS | | | | | | | | | | |
|---|---|---|---|---|---|---|---|---|---|---|---|---|---|
| | | | | | Compre-hension | | Format | | | | | | |
| | Content and Construct | Concurrent and Predictive | Justification | Item Relevance | Content | Instructions | Layout | Illustration/Print Quality | Auditory Presentation | Coherence | Response Mode | Recording Responses | Power Test |
| Rating Range ➡ | 0-8 | 0-4 | 0-1 | 0-1 | 0-2 | 0-4 | 0-1 | 0-1 | 0-1 | 0-1 | | 0-2 | 0-1 |
| C.  Recognition or Discrimination Tests (Continued) | | | | | | | | | | | | | |
| CYZYK PREREADING INVENTORY | 0 | 0 | 0 | 1 | 1 | 3 | 0 | 0 | 1 | 1 | Wr | 2 | 1 |
| HARRIS GRADED WORD TEST | 0 | 0 | 0 | 1 | 1 | 1 | 0 | 0 | 0 | 1 | Or | 2 | 1 |
| INDIVIDUAL READING PLACEMENT INVENTORY, Auditory Discrimination | 4 | 2 | 0 | 1 | 2 | 1 | 1 | 1 | 0 | 1 | Or | 2 | 1 |
| INDIVIDUAL READING PLACEMENT INVENTORY, Word Recognition | 4 | 2 | 0 | 1 | 1 | 1 | 1 | 1 | 0 | 1 | Or | 2 | 1 |
| INFORMAL READING INVENTORY, Visual & Auditory Perception & Discrimination | 0 | 0 | 0 | 1 | 2 | 1 | 1 | 0 | 0 | 1 | Or | 2 | 1 |
| INFORMAL READING INVENTORY, Word Recognition and Analysis | 0 | 0 | 0 | 1 | 1 | 1 | 1 | 0 | 0 | 1 | Or | 2 | 1 |
| READING EVALUATION - ADULT DIAGNOSIS Word Analysis | 2 | 0 | 0 | 1 | 2 | 1 | 1 | 1 | 0 | 1 | Or | 2 | 1 |
| READING EVALUATION - ADULT DIAGNOSIS Word Recognition | 2 | 0 | 0 | 1 | 2 | 1 | 1 | 1 | 0 | 1 | Or | 2 | 1 |
| | | | | | | | | | | | | | |
| D. Vocabulary Tests | | | | | | | | | | | | | |
| ADULT BASIC READING INVENTORY, Word Meaning ( Listening ) | 0 | 2 | 1 | 1 | 1 | 4 | 1 | 1 | 1 | 1 | Wr | 2 | 1 |
| ADULT BASIC READING INVENTORY, Word Meaning ( Reading ) | 1 | 2 | 1 | 1 | 1 | 4 | 1 | 1 | 1 | 1 | Wr | 2 | 1 |
| | | | | | | | | | | | | | |
| | | | | | | | | | | | | | |
| | | | | | | | | | | | | | |
| | | | | | | | | | | | | | |

Note:    The body of the table includes the ratings assigned to each test for individual criteria.
A figure of zero on any criterion indicates noncompliance or lack of information.

The meanings of the symbols under "Response Mode" are as follows:
"Or" — Oral;  "Wr" — Written; and "Mi" — Mixed.

TABLE 7. (Continued)

| TECHNICAL EXCELLENCE | | | | ADMINISTRATIVE USABILITY | | | | | | | | | | | | | | | | TOTAL GRADES |
|---|---|---|---|---|---|---|---|---|---|---|---|---|---|---|---|---|---|---|---|---|
| Reliability | | | | Administration | | | | | Interpretation | | | | | | | | | | | |
| Alternate Form | Test-Retest | Internal Consistency | Replicability | Training of Admin. | Admin. Time | Clarity of Manual | Number of Admin. | Scoring | Training | Range | Diversity | Score Conversion | Interpre | Real Life Skills | Validating Group | Racial/Ethnic/Sex Represent. | Can Decisions Be Made? | Alternate Forms | Form Comparability | TOTAL GRADES |
| 0-3 | 0-3 | 0-2 | 0-1 | 0-1 | 0-1 | 0-1 | 0-1 | 0-2 | 0-1 | 0-1 | 0-1 | 0-2 | 0-1 | 0-1 | 0-1 | 0-2 | 0-2 | 0-1 | 0-1 | Good-Fair-Poor |
| | | | | | | | | | | | | | | | | | | | | |
| 0 | 0 | 0 | 0 | 1 | 1 | 0 | 1 | 1 | 1 | 0 | 0 | 0 | 0 | 0 | 0 | 0 | 0 | 0 | 0 | PFPP |
| 0 | 0 | 0 | 0 | 1 | 1 | 0 | 1 | 2 | 1 | 1 | 0 | 2 | 1 | 0 | 0 | 0 | 1 | 0 | 0 | PPPP |
| 3 | 0 | 0 | 1 | 1 | 1 | 1 | 1 | 2 | 1 | 0 | 1 | 2 | 1 | 0 | 0 | 0 | 2 | 1 | 1 | FFFF |
| 3 | 0 | 0 | 1 | 1 | 1 | 1 | 1 | 1 | 1 | 1 | 1 | 1 | 1 | 0 | 0 | 0 | 2 | 1 | 1 | FFFF |
| 0 | 0 | 0 | 0 | 1 | 0 | 0 | 1 | 2 | 1 | 0 | 1 | 2 | 1 | 0 | 0 | 0 | 1 | 0 | 0 | PFPP |
| 0 | 0 | 0 | 0 | 1 | 0 | 0 | 1 | 2 | 1 | 0 | 1 | 2 | 1 | 0 | 0 | 0 | 1 | 0 | 0 | PFPP |
| 0 | 0 | 0 | 0 | 1 | 1 | 0 | 1 | 2 | 1 | 0 | 1 | 2 | 1 | 0 | 0 | 0 | 2 | 0 | 0 | PFPF |
| 0 | 0 | 0 | 0 | 1 | 1 | 0 | 1 | 2 | 1 | 0 | 1 | 2 | 1 | 0 | 0 | 0 | 2 | 0 | 0 | PFPF |
| | | | | | | | | | | | | | | | | | | | | |
| | | | | | | | | | | | | | | | | | | | | |
| 0 | 0 | 2 | 1 | 1 | 1 | 0 | 1 | 2 | 1 | 1 | 1 | 2 | 1 | 0 | 0 | 0 | 1 | 0 | 0 | PGFF |
| 0 | 0 | 2 | 1 | 1 | 1 | 0 | 1 | 2 | 1 | 1 | 1 | 2 | 1 | 0 | 0 | 0 | 2 | 0 | 0 | PGFF |
| | | | | | | | | | | | | | | | | | | | | |
| | | | | | | | | | | | | | | | | | | | | |
| | | | | | | | | | | | | | | | | | | | | |
| | | | | | | | | | | | | | | | | | | | | |
| | | | | | | | | | | | | | | | | | | | | |

The entries under Total Grades summarize test performance on the four major criterion areas, in this order: 1. Measurement Validity, 2. Examinee Appropriateness, 3. Technical Excellence, and 4. Administrative Usability. Thus, the entry "PGFF" is to be interpreted:

    Poor for Measurement Validity
    Good for Examinee Appropriateness
    Fair for Technical Excellence
    Fair for Administrative Usability

It is interesting to note that Nafziger, Thompson, Hiscox, and Owen do not rate any adult literacy tests as "good" in measurement validity. Not surprisingly, the tests which are rated most highly in this area are those in the criterion-referenced category. Although these tests are often difficult to administer and lack technical reliability data (largely, perhaps, because of their rather limited use), they tend best to measure the adult student's ability to cope with real-life reading needs. This type of test is thus most consistent with the manner in which literacy in the 1970s has been related to coping skills, especially in the Harris Associates and Adult Performance Level Studies described in chapter 1.

If formal testing must be employed, it should be directed at the adult student's capacity to comprehend real-life reading materials. Testing with materials which are not directly related to the student's real-life concerns *or* testing subskills which are not obviously and immediately relevant for this purpose is meaningless and may be unnecessarily demoralizing for undereducated adults. A criterion-reference emphasis, based upon real-life coping skills, is the appropriate focus for formal measurement directed toward placement and evaluation of learning progress. In regard to evaluation pertaining to the student's mastery of relevant intermediate subskills, we would attempt to accomplish this entirely through informal and unsystematic means.

# Conclusion

This chapter has called attention to some of the fallacies in common practice for evaluating the progress of adult remedial readers. In short, there is far too much emphasis on the use of standardized norm-referenced tests in attempts to evaluate instruction and learning related to specific life goals. Also, there is often a tendency by educators to allow tests to be the sole indicators of reading success when, in fact, tests are not designed to measure some of the most crucial program elements and student concerns.

The most meaningful assessments are conducted informally by teachers and individual students. Teachers should trust their basic instincts about student progress. Once a student adopts realistic expectations in regard to his learning rate, he too can effectively assess progress toward his personal reading goals.

Where specific analysis and instrumentation are employed in informal assessment procedures, these should be qualitative rather than quantitative and should focus on the effort to accentuate what the adult remedial reader *can* do rather than what he *can't*. Emphasis should be on overall meaning rather than decoding precision, and ultimately on silent rather than oral reading. Where teachers are required to employ formal testing for purposes of placement and evaluation of learning progress, these tests should be of the criterion-referenced variety. (See table 7.) They should also focus specifically on real-life reading matter.

# Chapter 9

# Writing in Support of Reading

The three phases of our reading-instruction program have presented our strategies for helping functional illiterates evolve from total unfamiliarity with print to the point of being able to read independently with some degree of success. As a supplement to "pure" reading instruction, the present chapter is concerned not only with the learner's ability to decode and comprehend written language but with his ability to produce it as well.

The strategies for writing described in this chapter are supportive of and related to reading instruction in various ways. These strategies are generally presented in ascending order of difficulty and extent of learner independence required. The dictation stage of letter writing, for example, is not only uncomplicated in terms of its demands upon the student but a logical extension of language-experience and assisted reading as discussed in Phase I. The point is that students need not be experienced readers before teachers introduce them to writing-related activities. The writing strategies presented in this chapter may be used to support reading activities or simply to teach writing itself, as teachers deem appropriate. Reading and writing are, for the most part, mutually supportive, in addition to the fact that each is a necessary survival skill in its own right.

At its most basic level, writing is a matter of penmanship. The learner copies letters and words which appear in print or have been written by someone else. This process, of course, requires considerable attention to detail, which inevitably adds to the student's consciousness of letter and word differences. This increased sensitivity to distinctive features be-

comes a crucial asset in word identification. As a consequence, teachers
may wish to experiment with teaching beginning writing in conjunction
with word-attack skills, as described in Phase II. Furthermore, by engaging in the "personalized" cloze and application activities described in the
next section, students not only combine reading and writing but reinforce
the distinctive features in the particular print which is of primary importance in their lives. As a result, because the personalized cloze and application activities involve the student in printing his name, address, place of
employment, etc., they strengthen his ability to recognize and produce
this information outside the classroom. Thus the mechanical process of
writing his personal "key words" contributes to the student's efforts to
achieve literacy.

When viewed as a means of converting one's thoughts to paper, writing
activities become an asset to reading comprehension. As he engages in
writing in response to reading (filling in blanks, completing open-ended
statements, or answering "thought questions"), the reader is forced to
organize his thoughts about written and printed materials. In letter writing
and more advanced forms of creative writing, he is encouraged to think in
terms of structure and organization. When he must focus upon organizing
his writing as meaningfully as possible, the student becomes more attuned
to the organizational patterns of text when he reads. The individual who
has struggled to communicate his thoughts on paper is more apt to think
globally with respect to someone else's writing. Such a reader can more
easily take advantage of advance organizers and think in terms of themes
and concepts needed for understanding.

The discussion of specific strategies will be subdivided under two sections: "Writing as a Reactor" and "Writing as an Initiator."

# Writing as a Reactor

Beginning writers require structure in which to work. The activities discussed in this section focus upon teaching the learner to write responses to
what he reads. In this manner, he is guided with respect to what he will
write or at least what he will write about. The major activities described
involve filling out standardized forms and responding to thought questions
provoked by text.

## Application and Related Activities

As indicated earlier, the first stage of writing development begins with a
purely mechanical emphasis. The adult student merely copies printing
that appears in a book or has been done by someone else. The most
practical material is, of course, that which most closely approximates the

learner's real-life writing demands. Ideally, the student should begin by copying his name, then focus upon his address, his place of employment, and other material which he is most likely to be called upon to reproduce. Once he succeeds in copying a few such "personalized" items legibly, he is ready to begin to write them from memory. This activity can be made even more "lifelike" when the student writes in response to what he has read. This is exactly what happens every time an individual is required to fill out an application or respond to any standardized form.

**Extended Rationale for Application Activities.** The typical adult is confronted with forms relating to a variety of purposes, including seeking employment, application for welfare or social security payments, application for medical benefits, loans, credit, etc. Although the required forms differ somewhat for these various purposes, they ask for a great deal of the same basic information. It is therefore particularly important not only that a student be able to recognize and discriminate among items that call for his name, address, occupation, marital status, references, etc., but that he be able to spell and write these items accurately and legibly.

Supervised practice with real applications provides the opportunity for the student to focus on the mutually supportive literacy skills of reading, writing, and spelling, while using materials which are personally and immediately relevant to his life requirements. The knowledge and abilities which he acquires are helpful to him, not just in filling out forms but in any situation where he finds it necessary to read and write basic information pertaining to his personal circumstances.

The application experience is an ongoing learning activity, each stage bringing the student closer to independence not only in working with applications but in his language-arts coping skills as a whole. It also serves as a focal point for a variety of related activities. The student may acquire valuable experience in seeking information he needs for an application. He can use the dictionary to help him spell and the telephone book to locate the addresses and phone numbers of his references. He has the further opportunity to check his own work, locating his spelling and punctuation errors, once he and the teacher have established a model to guide his work.

**Personalized Cloze.** We begin acclimating adult remedial learners to applications by having them respond to a structured cloze-type activity which calls for much of the same information required by most standardized forms. The advantage of using this procedure as a forerunner to the actual application process is that, in the case of the beginning reader, it not only acquaints him with many of the terms employed on applications (name, for example, or address) but allows him to encounter these terms first in a full written context. The novice reader is first presented with a passage such as the following:

MY NAME IS _____ _____ I LIVE ON _____ STREET (ROAD, AVENUE,
ETC.) IN THE CITY (TOWN) OF _____ IN THE STATE OF _____. MY DATE
OF BIRTH IS _____ AND I AM _____ YEARS OF AGE. I AM MARRIED TO
_____ AND MY CHILDREN'S NAMES ARE _____. I
WORK AT _____.

Passages such as the above may of course be adapted to accommodate the needs of specific individuals and student groups. Not all persons will be married, for example, but all will encounter the term *married* (or *marital status*) on forms to which they are asked to respond. Thus it is important that the individual be able to recognize this term in print, if only to respond that it is inapplicable in his case.

Beginning readers should be exposed to the personalized cloze in the same manner that they began assisted reading. The instructor reads a passage and pauses for the student to supply (orally) the missing words (or complete the statement) until the student is able to read the entire passage. He is then provided with a list of "personalized" key words to fill in the blanks. This list of items is presented in the same order as the blanks in the passage. Later, the order of the key words is scrambled, until finally the list is eliminated altogether, as the student becomes capable of filling in the blanks from memory.

When the individual becomes reasonably proficient with this exercise and familiar with different personalized cloze passages, he is ready for transition to a real-life application format.

**The Application Form.** Focus on application forms in an adult remedial classroom may begin in one of several ways. An adult student may bring to class an actual form which confronts him (a rent application, for example) and seek the teacher's assistance. Or a teacher may acquire job applications from local employers or construct simulated forms based on formats of applications for various purposes pertaining to student needs and interests (see figure 4).

As students are exposed to the application process, they are quick to recognize that this is an activity of real-life importance in which each individual is challenged to produce a unique product which presents a picture of himself. The student becomes aware that a real application is judged by prospective employers (or landlords, etc.) not only on its content but on its appearance as well. He can be encouraged to believe that, with practice in reading, spelling, penmanship, and the mechanics of appropriate punctuation and capitalization, he can learn to produce an application whose appearance advertises him well. At the same time, he acquires skills which will serve him effectively in life as a whole.

The student should not be confronted with the classroom task of filling out an application until he can read and write somewhat. Once he acquires

_____ 19___                          Please Attach
                                       Passport or
Application of                         Similar Photograph
    Mr.
    Mrs.
    Miss_____
    (If married, please give first name, and name before marriage)

Present Address _____ Phone _____

Permanent Address _____ Phone _____

Present Position _____ Soc. Sec. No. _____

_____

| School Attended | Dates of Attendance | | Diploma, Degree or Certificate |
|---|---|---|---|
| | From | To | |

Course or Specialty _____

Marital Status ___ Children ___ Height ___ Weight ___ Eyesight ___ Hearing ___

Other _____ Birth Date _____

Place of Birth _____ Church Preference _____

Present Salary _____ Least Salary You Will Accept _____

| Name and Address of Firm | Dates Employed | | Reason for Leaving |
|---|---|---|---|
| | From | To | |

| Reference Names | Complete Address | Title or Position |
|---|---|---|

Figure 4. Application for Employment

minimum literacy skills, however, he may be presented with a simplified application (usually a simulated form at this stage) and invited to do what he can. After the student has made the most of this initial effort at independence, he and his instructor may carefully read the application together, clarifying what information is called for. When the student is equipped to respond to all relevant items, he works individually again until he has done so. The teacher may then help him review and correct his responses, after which the student may fill out a duplicate form to reinforce what he has learned. This second form becomes instructional material for further refinement, and the cycle continues.

To avoid frustrating the student by demanding more of him than he can accomplish in his first exposure to the application activity, it is recommended that teachers focus upon only one of the following levels of "accuracy" at a time:

1. Meaningful responses are made to all appropriate application items.
2. Spelling is correct.
3. Punctuation and capitalization are correct.

The complete process of refining the student's application procedure involves a series of blank forms. Once the student demonstrates ability to fill out an application on which he supplies all the necessary information (an activity involving reading and writing), the teaching-learning focus may be shifted to spelling. After correcting his spelling errors on one application form, the student attempts a duplicate blank form. At this stage, his challenge is to respond appropriately to all items in correct spelling. The focus then shifts to punctuation and capitalization, where the teacher's assistance is required again, and a similar cycle follows until the student's application is completely "refined." The student is ready, at this point, to take on a more detailed application and/or a form with such directions as "Print name in full, last name first," rather than simply "Name."

It can be readily observed that the application procedure, as described above, includes little teaching in the customary sense. Rather, it is a series of refinements upon which teacher and student work together, but for which the student takes the major responsibility once he is equipped with the necessary prerequisites: the desire to fill out standardized forms accurately and neatly, plus the assistance of a resource person who will provide him with written models and answer his questions.

## Answering Questions

The first stage of our writing program also involves writing in response to contextual reading. In this instance the emphasis is not upon having the student respond to individual items on a standard form but upon having him write answers to questions about what he has read. Such questions not only give him the opportunity to express himself on paper but serve as an aid to comprehension by probing the student's reading reactions at various levels.

Different types of questions have been categorized by a number of authors according to different "comprehension levels." Many reading textbooks (Brunner and Campbell's *Participation in Secondary Reading,* for example) describe several taxonomies, all of which are similar in a number of respects. Whichever of these taxonomies is employed (Barrett, Herber, Ruddell, etc.), and whatever terminology used, it appears that there are at least three broad categories of questions for probing reading comprehension. Somewhat arbitrarily, we use the terms applied to questioning strategies associated with the Junior Great Books Reading and Discussion Program.

At the factual level of comprehension, the reader does not manipulate the ideas of the text but merely digests (with no conscious interpretation) the supposedly indisputable facts presented by the author. Literal comprehension (and acceptable answers to literal questions) are supposedly the same for all readers. Questions aimed at the literal level of comprehension might include such factual inquiries as "According to the author, what year was George Washington born?" or "What does the author say was the primary cause of the Civil War?" Questions of fact require the learner to offer quotations or paraphrases from the book to support his answers. All answers are "written down" in the selection.

Questions of interpretation require that the reader explore the author's meaning according to what he can infer from print. The reader offers his *opinions*, which he supports with *evidence* (as opposed to explicit statements) from the text. To stimulate critical thought, questions requiring interpretive comprehension may often be posed in "two-pronged" form, such as, "According to the author, was the Civil War fought primarily over the issue of slavery or the issue of states' rights?" (where the teacher wishes to stimulate the reader's comprehension of a chapter on the Civil War in which the author's views were not explicitly stated). This question forces the student to organize and defend his viewpoint, even if he doesn't believe, on the basis of his reading, that either slavery or states' rights is contended by the author to have been the primary issue behind the war. He is forced to focus upon what inferences, with regard to the author's viewpoint, might be justified in terms of what he has read.

Interpretive questions are of course not limited to "content" material such as the Civil War but apply perhaps more readily to fiction, as illustrated by the following examples:

1. According to the story "Christmas Is for Giving," is it more important to increase the length of life or to improve the quality of life? Why?
2. According to the story "The Blue Cup," is it always best to tell the whole truth? Justify your answer.

Each of the preceding is a basic question, potentially giving rise to a series of follow-up questions through which students may probe the author's meaning in a selection. Such questions may also be used by the teacher to promote student discussion and thus enhance comprehension, prior to having students write their answers.

Although the range of appropriate material for interpretive questions is not as broad as that for factual questions, there is a great deal of adult reading matter in which the reader is called upon to interpret the author's meaning and to make inferences of various kinds. With our more independent students, for example, we have often used selections from *The Readers Digest*, which tend to be relatively short and are apt to appeal to a diversity of student interests.

A third category of questions is those which are termed *evaluative* (or in other taxonomies *applicative*). Evaluative questions ask the student to determine the extent to which he agrees with the author's meaning and the extent to which the author's meaning has relevance in his own life. This category of questions thus draws not only upon the reader's background experience but upon his standards of value pertaining to truth, beauty, happiness, goodness, etc. Parallel to the examples presented above for interpretive questions, two evaluative questions (in response to the same stories) might be:

1. In your own mind, is it more important to increase the length of life or to improve the quality of life?
2. Do you believe it is always best to tell the whole truth?

The preceding overview of categories of questions to probe comprehension has not addressed the issue of where these questions fit in our reading/writing program. Logically, answering questions pertaining to reading matter is a step beyond the application process; even where reading matter is not difficult, a great deal more is expected of the learner. He must be much more analytical and creative.

Regardless of reading ability, we believe that writing answers to questions directed at all three comprehension levels is an important activity for adult remedial learners. As a reading-comprehension activity, it shows the student that the term *comprehension* (like the term *reading*) means different things at different times and that comprehension is highly personalized and, legitimately, may often vary among individuals. As a writing activity, answering interpretive and evaluative questions encourages the student to organize his thoughts according to unifying themes. If the student is forced to do this when he writes, he will be more apt to do it when he reads as well.

## Paraphrase

A good way to build upon the student's background knowledge in language experience and, at the same time, begin the process of teaching him to observe writing conventions is with the tool of *paraphrase.* In this activity the student listens to or reads an article, story, radio or television episode, etc., and either dictates or writes down (in his own words, depending on his ability level) what happened. With the paraphrase activity, then, the student uses his own knowledge of oral language to express himself in written form; however, in recording content expressed by others, he must pay attention to the language and sentence structure of speakers or writers in order to represent their statements accurately. He is therefore exposed to some of the language conventions which may be unfamiliar to him and he begins to adopt them in the context of his own expression.

Students who are able may write their own paraphrases and those who are learning basic penmanship may copy paraphrases that have been recorded by the teacher. In either case, the student is involved in a profitable "intermediate" activity which builds upon his own language, yet reinforces the grammar and syntax of standard written English. This experience will serve him well as he begins to write letters and other "creative" material.

# Writing as an Initiator

Whereas the activities in the previous section involve the student in responding in writing to material he has read, the next set of activities focuses primarily upon writing as a means of communication. It is still true, however, that these "initiator" writing activities relate to reading in several important ways. In letter writing, the major activity discussed in this section, beginning readers may use their dictated letters as reading material (as in language-experience and assisted reading). Furthermore, the efforts to read and to write are mutually supportive for many learners. At a word-recognition level, the effort to *produce* letters and words reinforces the beginning reader's effort to recognize their appearance in print. At a comprehension level, the effort to organize main ideas for writing purposes makes the beginning reader more conscious of looking for organization in print which has been produced by others.

## Letter Writing

The opportunity to dictate and eventually to write his own letters provides the adult remedial student with a language experience which offers an especially gratifying reward. The letter-writing enterprise not only strengthens the student's reading and writing but equips him to perform a practical and necessary life skill. Since many students have never written a letter, or even considered the possibility that they are capable of doing so, this activity offers a substantial morale boost as well.

**Rationale for Letter Writing.** The rationale for letter writing as an instructional device in the teaching of reading is an extension of language experience as a whole. The student's reading potential is maximized when he is able to conceptualize print as "talk written down." In reading letters he has created himself, the student is dealing with his own language and his own speaking vocabulary. Also, since he is expressing thoughts and using terms in which he has personal investment, he has added advantage and incentive in reading his own creations.

Although basically a language-experience activity, letter writing has an added dimension. The student produces material which is intended to convey a specific message to someone else. He is thus encouraged to pay particular attention to the organization of his thoughts, which he can reanalyze as he reads them. This process is a much stiffer challenge than dictation of simple "episodes," required at the beginning of the language-experience approach to reading instruction.

**The Letter-writing (and -reading) Process.** The prospect of writing his own letters is usually quite appealing to the functionally illiterate adult, once he is convinced that this is a task he can actually perform. Although he may have to prod in the beginning, the sensitive teacher can usually elicit from the student the name of someone to whom he'd like to write. This will frequently be an out-of-town friend or relative, but occasionally the student may wish to write a more formal letter relating to a personal concern of a business or political nature. In any case, the teacher begins by showing the student a model of a letter that is appropriate for his objective. Such models are available from a variety of sources. They are sometimes included in Adult Basic Education kits and workbooks, or teachers may locate these formats in high school English texts or create them themselves.

After he has been exposed to the format of the letter he will compose, the student dictates information for the heading, the name for the salutation, then the body of the letter. Because he is unaccustomed to letter composition, he often needs to be stimulated with such basic questions as "What else can you tell him about that?" or "What has happened to you lately that is unusual?" (If he is writing a formal letter which requires an "inside address," the student must acquire this information in advance.) After the letter has been dictated and recorded, it is read aloud for the student's approval. Then, after the letter is typed (preferably before the next class), the student and teacher review it together, using the assisted reading technique. The student continues to review his letter alone until he can read it independently and fluently.

Once the adult remedial student is able to read his letter without assistance, he may practice copying it in his own handwriting. This exercise involves making the transition from typed print to formation of letters and words in the writer's own cursive style. For beginning students, this is much more difficult than it sounds, but it may be worthwhile for several reasons. It helps to strengthen the mutually supportive relationships among reading, writing, and spelling. Furthermore, it brings the student a step closer to his goal of being able to produce written compositions independently.

As the adult student grows in his ability to dictate and read his own letters, he approaches the challenge of committing his message directly to paper. At this stage, the perceptive teacher is not overly concerned about mechanics—not until the student has the opportunity to organize his thoughts and write them down. After the student has completed his initial writing effort, there is ample opportunity to help him perform the editorial function of correcting spelling and punctuation.

Upon completion of repeated reading and rewriting, the student places the letter in an envelope and addresses, stamps, and mails it. Eventually he may receive a reply, which provides additional reading matter of high personal interest.

## Creative Writing

We will comment only briefly on creative writing as a logical ultimate step in "Writing as an Initiator." While teaching creative writing is certainly not a major thrust of literacy training, it is important to remember that persons who are limited in their literacy skills have no necessary restrictions on their creativity. Often, in fact, the incentive for creativity becomes the spark which inspires an individual to push harder with his literacy effort as a whole. As a consequence, the important thing about creative writing in literacy classes is that it be enjoyable. Often it can be conducted as a recreational break from the more intense study involved in such activities as word-identification skills or filling in applications.

Probably the form of creative writing most suitable for remedial reading and literacy classes is poetry, which offers a variety of structures and forms amenable to collaborative or individual class activity. Furthermore, numerous works may be produced in a single session, a potential which is impossible with most other literary forms.

To produce poetry, students need a structure and ideas. Both may be provided by the right kinds of advance organizers. As a beginning exercise, for example, a class of adults may be asked to complete the same line, such as:

WHEN I WAS A CHILD . . .

The resulting collection of lines, when recorded by the teacher on the chalkboard, is a poem which may also be treated as a language-experience/ assisted reading activity for students in Phase I of their reading development. Any number of similar "starters" may be devised, either for individuals or groups, such as, "I wish I had" or "I remember when" or "I used to, but now . . ."

As another type of exercise, interested students might be asked to focus on colors or dreams or noises or any number of topics teachers and/or students may devise. In teaching poetry in a nursing home, Kenneth Koch (1977) directed his students about colors as follows: "Think of your favorite color or a color you like a lot and write about what it makes you think of. Put the name of the color, if you like, in every line or so" (p. 22). One of the poems elicited, which accepts this suggestion, is:

> My brain is red
> My dress is red
> My hair is red
> Lord have mercy on me
> The pomegranates in the Barbodes
>     are red inside
> And sweet
> And you know something?
> I used to go pick them off people's trees
> But I didn't like them
> I picked them just for a joke
> And they put me in jail.
> And gave me a whipping
>
> —Merriam Sullivan

In response to the topic "touch," another student wrote:

> A string of beads
> They feel like pearls
> Like a woman wears
>     around her neck
> When she goes out to
>     wedding and parties.
> They look like wood
> And they're hard.
>
> —Harry Siegel

This brief section is intended merely as an introduction to some of the ways in which writing poetry, as either an individual or a group activity, may be introduced into literacy classes. Through these activities students are both—and often simultaneously—writing reactors and writing initiators. Much of our discussion and all our examples have been derived from two excellent books by Kenneth Koch, *Wishes, Lies, and Dreams* and *I Never Told Anybody (Teaching Poetry Writing in a Nursing Home)*. We recommend them to anyone interested in developing poetry activities for literacy classes.

# Bibliography

Alexander, K. "The Value of an Education," *Journal of Education Finance* (1976), 1(4); 429, 467.

Auckerman, R. L. *Approaches to Beginning Reading.* New York: John Wiley, 1971.

Barnett, T. L., and Smith, R. J. *Teaching Reading in the Middle Grades.* Reading, Mass.: Addison-Wesley, 1974.

Bernstein, B. "Social Class, Speech Systems and Psychotherapy." In F. Reissman, J. Cohen, and A. Pearl, *Mental Health of the Poor.* New York: Free Press of Glencoe, 1964.

Bosco, J. A. "Levels of Abstraction and the Adult Reader," *Adult Literacy and Basic Education* (1977), 1(3): 54–66.

Bowren, F. R., and Zintz, M. V. *Teaching Reading in Adult Basic Education.* Dubuque, Iowa: William C. Brown Co., 1977.

Brunner, J. F., and Campbell, J. J. *Participating in Secondary Reading: A Practical Approach.* Englewood Cliffs, N.J.: Prentice-Hall, 1978.

Burke, C. L., and Goodman, Y. M. *Reading Miscue Inventory Manual Procedure for Diagnosis and Evaluation.* New York: Macmillan, 1972.

*CBS News Almanac* (1978 ed.). Maplewood, N.J.: Hammond Almanac, 1977.

Ciardi, J. *How Does a Poem Mean?* Boston: Houghton Mifflin, 1959.

Bierdiansky, B., Cronnell, B. and Koehler, J. A. *Spelling-Sound Relations and Primary Form — Class Descriptions for Speech — Comprehension Vocabulary of 6–9 Year Olds.* Technical Report No. 15. Southwest Regional Laboratory for Educational Research and Development, 1969.

Coles, G. S. "U.S. Literacy Statistics: How to Succeed with Hardly Trying," *Literacy Work* (1976), 5(2): 47–70.

Cook, W. D. *Adult Literacy Education in the United States.* Newark, Del.: International Reading Association, 1977.

Cooper, C. R., and Petrosky, A. R. "A Psycholinguistic View of the Fluent Reading Process," *Journal of Reading* (1976), 20(3): 184–206.

Cunningham, P. M., Arthur, S. V., and Cunningham, J. W. *Classroom Reading Instruction: Alternative Approaches.* Lexington, Mass.: D. C. Health, 1977.

Darkenwald, G. C. *Some Effects of the "Obvious Variable": Teacher's Race and Holding Power with Black Adult Students.* New York: Center for Adult Education, Columbia University Teachers College, 1974.

Dinnan, J. *Teaching Reading to the Disadvantaged Adult.* Englewood Cliffs, N.J.: Prentice-Hall, 1971.

Dolch, E. W. *The Basic Sight Word Test.* Champaign, Ill.: Garrard, 1942 (chap. 8).

Durkin, D. "Children Who Read before Grade One," *Reading Teacher* (1961), 14(3): 163–66.

Erickson, E. H. *Childhood and Society.* 2d ed. New York: W. W. Norton, 1963.
_____. *Identity: Youth and Crisis.* New York: W. W. Norton, 1968.

Farr, R. "Keynote Address," Virginia State Reading Association Annual Conference, Roanoke, Va., April 1977.

Forrester, A. D. "What Teachers Can Learn from Natural Readers," *Reading Teacher* (1977), 30(2): 154–60.

Frandson, M. E. *"The Application of Selected Reference Groups' Concepts to the Analysis of Adult Education Enrollment"* (doctoral dissertation, University of California, 1970). Dissertation Abstracts International, 1970, 31, 1565A (University Microfilms No. 70-19,848).

Gibb, J. R. "Learning Theory in Adult Education." In M. S. Knowles (ed.), *Handbook of Adult Education in the United States.* Washington, D.C.: Adult Education Association of the U.S.A., 1960.

Giles, W. E., and Conti, G. J. "Poverty's Cause-Effect: Attacking Both through Lifelong Learning." In Donald P. Garner (ed.), *The Adult Learner, the World of Work, and Career Education.* The Career Educator, v.3. Dubuque, Iowa: Kendall/Hunt Publishing Co., 1978.

Gordon, J. E. "Counseling the Disadvantaged Boy." In W. E. Amos and J. D. Grambs (eds.), *Counseling the Disadvantaged Youth.* Englewood Cliffs, N.J.: Prentice-Hall, 1968.

Hampton, L. A., and Ashton, D. "Can We Reach the Urban Disadvantaged Adult?" *Journal of Extension* (1979), 17(4).

Harris, L., and Associates. *Survival Literacy Study.* New York: Harris and Associates, Inc., 1970 (ERIC Document Reproduction Service No. ED 068 813).
_____. *The 1971 National Reading Difficulty Index: A Study of Functional Reading Ability in the U.S. for the National Teaching Center.* New York: Harris and Associates, 1971 (ERIC Document Reproduction Service No. ED 057 312).

Harris, L. A., and Smith, C. B. *Reading Instruction: Diagnostic Teaching in the Classroom.* New York: Holt, Rinehart and Winston, 1976.

Havighurst, R. J. *Developmental Tasks and Education.* New York: David McKay Co., 1961.

Herber, H. L. *Teaching Reading in Content Areas.* Englewood Cliffs, N.J.: Prentice-Hall, 1970.

Hoskisson, K. "Assisted Reading and Parent Involvement," *Reading Teacher* (1974), 27(7).

————— and Krohm, B. "Reading by Immersion: Assisted Reading," *Elementary English* (1974), 51(6): 832–36.

Houle, C. O. *The Design of Education.* San Francisco: Jossey-Bass, 1972.

Hunter, C. S., and Harman, D. *Adult Illiteracy in the United States.* New York: McGraw-Hill, 1979.

Hurlock, E. B. *Developmental Psychology.* 4th ed. New York: McGraw-Hill, 1975.

Jhin, K. R. "National Challenge: 54,000,000 Adults with Less than a High School Diploma," *Adult Literacy and Basic Education* (1977), 1(2): 5–13.

Johnson, D. D., and Pearson, P. D. *Teaching Reading Vocabulary.* New York: Holt, Rinehart and Winston, 1978.

Kerckhoff, A. L., and Campbell, R. E. "Black-White Differences in the Educational Attainment Process," *Sociology of Education* (1977), 50(1): 15–27.

Knowles, M. S. *The Modern Practice of Adult Education: Andragogy versus Pedagogy.* New York: Association Press, 1970.

Knox, A. B. *Adult Development and Learning.* San Francisco: Jossey-Bass, 1977.

Koch, K. *I Never Told Anybody: Teaching People in a Nursing Home to Write Poetry.* New York: Vintage Books, 1977.

—————. *Wishes, Lies, and Dreams: Teaching Children to Write Poetry.* New York: Vintage Books, 1970.

Kolers, P. A. "Three Stages of Reading." In Frank Smith (ed.), *Psycholinguistics and Reading.* New York: Holt, Rinehart and Winston, 1973.

Landsman, T. "The Role of the Self Concept in Learning Situations," *High School Journal* (1962), 45: 289–95.

Literacy Volunteers of America, Inc. *1978 Annual Report.* Syracuse, N.Y.: Literacy Volunteers of America, 1978.

—————, and Hagstrom, W. O. *Adult Education and Social Class.* Berkeley: Survey Research Center, University of California, 1963.

London, J., and Wenkert, R. "Obstacles to Blue Collar Participation in Adult Education." In A. B. Shostak and W. Gomberg (eds.), *Blue Collar World: Studies of the American Worker.* Englewood Cliffs, N.J.: Prentice-Hall, 1964.

Lusterman, S. *Education in Industry* (Conference Board Report). New York: Conference Board, 1977.

McCoy, V. R. "Adult Life Cycle Change," *Lifelong Learning: The Adult Years* (1977), 1(2): 14–15.

McCracken, R. A. "Initiating Sustained Silent Reading," *Journal of Reading* (1971), 14(8): 521–24.

Mikulecky, L. J., Shanklin, N. L., and Caverly, D. C. *Adult Reading Habits, Attitudes, and Motivations: A Cross Sectional Study.* Monograph in Language and Reading Studies. Bloomington, Ind.: University of Indiana, 1979.

Miller, G. A., Brunner, J. S., and Postman, L. "Familiarity of Letter Sequences and Tachistoscopic Identification," *Journal of General Psychology* (1954), 50: 129–39.

Miller, S. M. "The American Lower Classes: A Typological Approach," *Sociology and Social Research* (1964), 31(1): 1–22.

Moore, W. M., Virginia Department of Education, Personal communication, Nov. 14, 1977.

Mosby, R. S. *Challenge to Society: The Education of the Culturally Disadvantaged Child.* A Seminar for Teachers of the Culturally Disadvantaged, v.3. New York: Pageant, 1971.

Moss, D., and Richardson, R. *A Study of Students Who Discontinued Attendance in the ESEA III Adult Basic Education Program.* New York: New York City Board of Education, June 1967 (ERIC Document Reproduction Service No. ED 019 576).

Nafziger, D. H., Thompson, R. B., Hiscox, M., and Owen, T. R. *Tests of Functional Adult Literacy: An Evaluation of Currently Available Instruments.* Portland, Ore.: Northwest Regional Educational Laboratory, 1975.

National Advisory Council for Adult Education. *1977 Annual Report.* Washington, D.C.: U.S. Government Printing Office, 1977.

National Affiliation for Literacy Advance. Personal communication, Nov. 1978.

*Newsweek,* Nov. 6, 1978, pp. 106–10.

Northcott, N. "Functional Literacy for Adults: A Status Report of the Adult Performance Level Study." Paper presented at Annual Meeting of the International Reading Association, New Orleans, May 1–4, 1974 (ERIC Document Reproduction Service ED 091 672).

Northcott, N., and others. *Adult Functional Competency: A Summary.* Austin: University of Texas at Austin, Division of Extension, 1975.

O'Donnell, M. P. *Teaching Reading to the Untaught.* New York: Multi-Media Education, Inc., 1975.

Orem, R. C. "Language and the Culturally Disadvantaged." In W. E. Amos and J. D. Grambs (eds.), *Counseling the Disadvantaged Youth.* Englewood Cliffs, N.J.: Prentice-Hall, 1968.

Park, R. "Trends in ABE: A Little Competency-based Caution," *ABE Network News* (1979). 3(4): 1, 5.

Patterson, O. "Functional Adult Literacy." In *Projections for Reading: Preschool through Adulthood.* Washington, D.C.: U.S. Government Printing Office, 1977.

Pearson, P. D., and Johnson, D. D. *Teaching Reading Comprehension.* New York: Holt, Rinehart and Winston, 1978.

Peck, R. C. "Psychological Developments in the Second Half of Life." In J. E. Anderson (ed.), *Psychological Aspects of Aging.* Washington, D.C.: American Psychological Association, 1956.

Peterson, R. E., and others. *Toward Lifelong Learning in America: A Sourcebook for Planners.* Berkeley, Calif.: Educational Testing Service, 1979.

Prins, J. V. "A Study to Determine Reasons Adults Drop Out of an Adult Basic Education Literacy Program" (doctoral dissertation, Wayne State University, 1972). Dissertation Abstracts International 1972, 33, 2063A (University Microfilms No. 72-28, 475).

Puder, W. H., and Hand, S. F. "Personality Factors Which May Interfere with Learning of Adult Education Students," *Adult Education* (1969) 18(2): 81–93.

Richardson, D. C., and Nyer, L. M. *Participation in Texas Programs of Adult Basic Education: An Identification and Analysis of Factors Related to Rates of Enrollment, Attendance, and Completion in Adult Basic Education.* Austin: Texas Department of Community Affairs, Office of Education, Information, and Training, October 1974 (ERIC Document Reproduction Service No. ED 099 662).

Ruddell, R. B. *Reading-Language Instruction: Innovative Practices.* Englewood Cliffs, N.J.: Prentice-Hall, 1974.

Ryan, W. *Blaming the Victim.* New York: Random House, 1971.

Samples, B. *The Metaphoric Mind.* Reading, Mass.: Addison-Wesley, 1976.

Schneiderman, P. "Without Reading You Ain't Nothing," *Lifelong Learning: The Adult Years* (1977), 1(1): 16–18.

Schroeder, W. L. "Adult Education Defined and Described." In R. M. Smith, G. F. Aku, and J. R. Kidd (eds.), *Handbook of Adult Education.* New York: Macmillan, 1970.

Smith, E., and Martin, M. *Guide to Curricula for the Disadvantaged Adult Programs.* Englewood Cliffs. N.J.: Prentice-Hall, 1972.

Smith, F. *Understanding Reading.* New York: Holt, Rinehart and Winston, 1971.

————. *Psycholinguistics and Reading.* New York: Holt, Rinehart and Winston, 1973.

————. *Comprehension and Learning.* New York: Holt, Rinehart and Winston, 1975.

————. *Understanding Reading.* 2d ed. New York: Holt, Rinehart and Winston, 1978.

Spache, G. D., and Spache, E. B. *Reading in the Elementary School.* Boston: Allyn and Bacon, 1977.

Stauffer, John. "Illiteracy in the United States: The Move to Voluntarism," *Literacy Discussion* (1973), 4(3): 251–83.

Stauffer, R. G. *Directing the Reading-Thinking Process.* New York: Harper and Row, 1975.

Torrey, J. W. "Learning to Read without a Teacher." In F. Smith (ed.), *Psycholinguistics and Reading.* New York: Holt, Rinehart and Winston, 1973.

Ulmer, C. *Teaching the Culturally Disadvantaged.* Englewood Cliffs, N.J.: Prentice-Hall, 1972.

U.S. Bureau of the Census. *Census of the Population: 1970* (Subject Reports, Final Report PC (2)-5 B, *Educational Attainment*). Washington, D.C.: U.S. Government Printing Office, 1973.

U.S. Office of Education, Department of Health, Education, and Welfare. *Adult Basic Education—Meeting the Challenge of the 1970's.* First Annual Report of National Advisory Committee on Adult Basic Education to the President of the United States and the Secretary of Health, Education, and Welfare (ERIC Document Reproduction Service No. ED 023 054).

————. *Evaluation of the Community-based Right-to-Read Program.* Berkeley, Calif.: Pacific Training and Technical Assistance Corp.; 1974.

Virginia State Department of Education. *The State of the Art of Reading in Virginia.* Richmond: State Department of Education, 1976.

West, E. M. "The Use of an Unobtrusive Screening Device to Approximate Reading Levels of Adults." In P. D. Pearson and J. Hansen (eds.), *Reading: Disciplined Inquiry in Process and Practice*. Clemson, S.C.: National Reading Conference, Inc., 1978.

Wilson, R. C. *The Use of the Adjective Check List to Describe the Adult Basic Education Student*. Manhattan: Kansas State University, 1975 (ERIC Document Reproduction Service No. ED 106 541).

Zahn, J. E. "Differences between Adults and Youth Affecting Learning" (unpublished manuscript, University of California [Berkeley] Education Extension, 1967).

# Index

Composed by Linguatype, Chicago, in Alphatype Caledo with
Century Schoolbook display type

Printed on 60-pound Warren's 66, a pH-neutral stock, and
bound by Braun-Brumfield, Inc.